MW00682242

The Novalis Guide
to Canadian Shrines

The Novalis Guide
to Canadian Shrines

Leonard St. John

NOVALIS

© 2002 Novalis, Saint Paul University, Ottawa, Canada

Cover design and layout: Caroline Gagnon
Cover photographs: St. Joseph's Oratory, Montreal (left); Shrine of Our
Lady of Guadalupe, Johnstown, NS (top right); Shrine of Our Lady of
Lourdes, Kronau, SK (bottom right)

Business Office:
Novalis
49 Front Street East, 2nd Floor
Toronto, Ontario, Canada
M5E 1B3

Phone: 1-800-387-7164 or (416) 363-3303
Fax: 1-800-204-4140 or (416) 363-9409
E-mail: cservice@novalis.ca

National Library of Canada Cataloguing in
Publication Data

St. John, Leonard
    The Novalis guide to Canadian shrines /
Leonard St. John. — 2nd ed.

Includes bibliographical references and index.
ISBN 2-89507-250-7

    1. Christian shrines–Canada–
Guidebooks. I. Title.

BX2320.5.C3S24 2002   263'.04271   C2002-901311-9

Printed in Canada.

All rights reserved. No part of this publication may be reproduced, stored
in a retrieval system, or transmitted in any form, or by any means,
electronic, mechanical, photocopying, recording, or otherwise, without
the written permission of the publisher.

All photographs that appear in this book are courtesy of the shrines they
illustrate and are reprinted with permission. All rights reserved.

We acknowledge the financial support of the Government of Canada
through the Book Publishing Industry Development Program (BPIDP)
for our publishing activities.

10 9 8 7 6 5 4 3 2 1   10 09 08 07 06 05 04 03 02

Table of Contents

Preface

The *Novalis Guide to Canadian Shrines* was written for people interested in going on pilgrimage as well as for arm-chair travelers. Its aim is to provide readers with enough information on individual shrines so they can decide on the ones they may wish to visit. A second aim is to introduce readers to pilgrimage lore and tradition.

The coverage of the shrines was intended to be wide-ranging if not comprehensive. Since it would be unmanageable to list every parish side altar, outdoor grotto, Calvary or wayside cross, these were left out (except for a few scattered examples to remind readers that these are legitimate types of shrines).

Entries are arranged geographically by province, and then, within each province, alphabetically by city, town or village. Entries include location, history and a description of the shrine, as well as practical information useful to the pilgrim. Because shrine devotions and activities do change, it is wise for the reader to contact the shrine for its most recent schedule before going on pilgrimage. In French Canada, only the larger shrines offer services in English. But even at a medium-sized shrine, an anglophone group having a bilingual member and accompanied by a priest should have no problem. In English Canada, services to francophone pilgrims are available mainly at shrines that have a French tradition, such as Midland, Ste. Anne des Chênes and Lac Ste. Anne.

I would like to thank the directors of the shrines who provided me with information. Thanks also go to the many priests and sisters at Deschâtelets Residence in Ottawa, whose suggestions over the meal table helped me to track down so many shrines. I would like to express appreciation to Father John Vandenakker of Ottawa for information on pilgrimages, Guy Laperrière of the University of Sherbrooke for his information on Quebec shrines, Heather Leier and Joseph Lozinsky for information on Saskatchewan shrines, Michael O'Hearn, Caryl

Green and the staff of Novalis for their suggestions, and Zony Wong and Germaine Blais for their assistance with typing. Finally, I would like to thank the staffs of Saint Paul University Library, the Oblate Archives, the National Library of Canada, University of Ottawa Library, the Ottawa Public Library, and all those who provided photographs.

Introduction

I. A Brief History of Pilgrimages

The Early Christian Church

Jerusalem, built as a city
which is bound firmly together,
to which the tribes go up,
the tribes of the Lord,
as was decreed for Israel,
to give thanks to the name of the Lord.
(Psalm 122:3, 4)

The Christian tradition of pilgrimage finds its roots in the Jewish tradition. At the time of Christ, the Jewish people visited the tombs of holy people and had many sanctuaries where healings occurred. But their great shrine was the Temple in Jerusalem. Christ himself made the pilgrimage to Jerusalem for the Feast of Passover and other festivals. By the second century, pilgrimages to the holy places associated with Christ's life were not yet common. They were also conducted in private for fear of Roman persecution.

In the 4th century Emperor Constantine and his mother, Helena, built large basilican churches at the sites of the Holy Sepulchre, the Ascension and the Nativity. This led to a large increase in the number of pilgrimages to the Holy Land from all over the Roman Empire. For the first time these pilgrimages were public rather than private.

In the meantime, pilgrims had begun travelling to Rome to the tombs of Saints Peter and Paul. In the 4th century Constantine built basilican churches over these tombs, Helena built the Basilica of the Holy Cross and Pope Damasus restored the graves of the martyrs in the catacombs. With the rise of monasticism in 4th-century Egypt, many pilgrims found their way into the Egyptian deserts to seek counsel from the Desert Fathers and

Mothers. By the 5th century the city of Constantinople had many Marian pilgrimage churches.

The Early Middle Ages

In Rome many of the graves of the early martyrs were located in catacombs outside the city walls. Christians, fearing the desecration of these graves during the barbarian invasions, transferred the bones to designated churches inside the walls. Some pilgrims were able to procure parts of these relics for local shrines in their homelands and, thus, new local pilgrimages emerged.

In the early Middle Ages pilgrimages declined in the western world, except among the Irish. The Muslim invasions of the Middle East and North Africa put a stop to a number of pilgrimages there. In the 11th century the first Crusade was launched because a fanatical Muslim Shiite sect began attacking pilgrims en route to the Holy Land and even destroyed the Holy Sepulchre.

The Later Middle Ages

The later Middle Ages proved to be a golden age of pilgrimage and at almost any given time large numbers of men and women were to be found on the road to shrines in Rome, Spain, Switzerland or even Jerusalem. Pilgrimages had an enormous impact on the exchange of ideas and the enrichment of European culture. Rulers began to improve highways and hostels for the pilgrims. Orders such as the Knights Templars and various religious confraternities were set up to help the poorer pilgrims. They defended the travellers from armed attack, ran hostels for the weary and hospitals for the sick. In 1300 Pope Boniface VIII proclaimed a Year of the Jubilee during which huge numbers of pilgrims visited the major basilicas of Rome. This celebration, in imitation of the ancient Hebrew Jubilee, remains today as the Holy Year that is celebrated every 25 years.

Pilgrims

The word "pilgrim" means traveller, especially a traveller to a holy place. It comes from the Latin *peregrinus*, which once meant a stranger, particularly a stranger in Rome.

When individuals became overwhelmed with the petty conflicts and ingrown guilts of their surroundings, a pilgrimage offered them a sense of escape and freedom. But the pilgrim's journey, especially if it was a long one, could be filled with

hazards such as robbery, physical violence and even epidem-
ics. Sea voyages were perhaps the worst. At sea, pilgrims faced
the danger of capture, death or enslavement at the hands of
Turkish or Barbary pirates.

It is no wonder, then, that prior to leaving on pilgrimage,
pilgrims made their wills and settled their worldly affairs. Nor
is it surprising that they went through a formal ceremony of
blessing their apparel and receiving the pilgrim's staff and scrip.
This ceremony, imitating the dubbing of a knight, made them
members of a new class, at least temporarily.

The pilgrim of the late Middle Ages wore distinctive cloth-
ing: a cape, a hood and a broad-brimmed hat turned up at the
front or back. Pilgrims each carried a staff, satchel and water
bottle. Plodding along at the rate of 18 to 20 miles a day, they
were entitled to shelter, heat and water at hostels and monasteries regularly spaced along the way. To claim these privileges
pilgrims carried a testimonial letter from their bishop. Medieval pilgrims customarily returned home with a badge as proof
that they had visited a specific shrine; for example, scallop shells
gathered from the beaches near the Shrine of St. James of
Compostella in Spain, or metal badges with the figure of a saint
on them. The scallop shell eventually became the symbol of all
pilgrims and was worn on the hat, shoulders or chest.

Holy Poverty

In the early Middle Ages pilgrimage as a form of piety was
influenced by monasticism and the idea that salvation could
be gained by giving up the material world. Later, many itinerant merchants completely changed their lives to become permanent pilgrims going from shrine to shrine begging alms,
modelling the pilgrim's life and even preaching. In western
Europe these people were called peregrinantes, and in Russia,
startsy. Not everyone chose to follow the rule of holy poverty,
however, and many royalty gained notoriety for the lavishness
of their entourage while on pilgrimage.

Penitence

From the beginning, most pilgrims travelled to a sanctuary
to do penance for their sins. In the 9th century the Church made
the pilgrimage a formal part of the penitential system. Indul-
gences were offered for particular pilgrimages as added incen-
tives. For certain crimes, such as murder and heresy, the peni-
tent, instead of being excommunicated or exiled, was forced to

do public penance and endure the hardships of the longer pilgrimages to Rome or Jerusalem. The temporary removal of the criminal from the scene of the crime, while preventing family feuds, often created unexpected problems for other pilgrims.

A vow to make a pilgrimage for one's sins was taken seriously. When some people realized that they could not fulfill their vow because of sickness or old age, they would pay a friend or relative to make the pilgrimage for them. But there were abuses even in this. Isabel of Bavaria, Queen of France, became notorious for hiring professional pilgrims and sending them to shrines all over Europe.

Pilgrims had many penitential-like customs. Upon reaching the *mons gaudii*, the hill of rejoicing from which they caught first sight of the shrine, pilgrims took up a penitential posture. Penitential exercises included giving alms or begging, making all-night vigils on the eve of a saint's feast day, climbing staircases on the knees, circling the outside of a church while saying special prayers, following a tile maze that symbolized the road to salvation, and visiting a particular series of churches, such as the seven basilicas of Rome.

Aim of a Pilgrimage

Different pilgrims had different aims. While some came to do penance for their sins, others came to gain an indulgence or simply to improve their spiritual lives. Some made the trip because of a promise to God or a saint for a favour received. These pilgrims often brought an *ex-voto* or gift that was placed in the shrine as a witness to the favour received: for example, a crutch or brace, a homemade painting of a healing or a favourite piece of jewellery.

Some pilgrims came to a shrine known for cures expecting to be healed during or after the pilgrimage. Others came to pray for favours at the tomb or relic of a saint. Still others came to pray in front of a miraculous picture or on the site of apparitions and other miraculous occurrences. As Chaucer's portraits of pilgrims in *The Canterbury Tales* suggest, not every pilgrim had sincere motives.

Reformation Period

At the beginning of the 16th century the number of pilgrims began to decline. Like many of the popular devotions, the pilgrimage was criticized by the Protestant reformers and discarded. It survived in Europe not because Catholic apologists defended it successfully but because it grew out of the faith of ordinary people. As such it was never fully under the control of the Church anyway. The best the Church could ever do was try to channel it in the right direction.

The Protestant Reformation resulted in the destruction of many shrines in northern Europe: for example, Glastonbury, Walsingham and the tomb of Becket at Canterbury. After the Catholic revival at the end of the 16th century, new shrines in far-flung parts of the world began to attract pilgrims: for example, Our Lady of Guadalupe in Mexico and the tomb of St. Francis Xavier in Goa, India.

More than ever before, the Catholic Church enlisted artists in support of pilgrimages. Seventeenth-century Rome was transformed by the baroque genius of Bernini and Borromini. In the 18th century, artists such as Balthasar Neumann, the Zimmerman brothers, and Egid Quirin Asam produced a whole series of spectacular pilgrimage churches in southern Germany. The finest artists were induced to decorate new altars and create elaborate reliquaries. In Brazil the great sculptor Aleijadinho did his best work for the Way of the Cross and sanctuary at Congonhas. In Austria Haydn wrote his *Missa Cellensis in C* for the shrine at Mariazell, while Mozart wrote his joyous *Coronation Mass* to commemorate the crowning of a picture of the Virgin at the shrine of Maria Plain.

Modern Period

Pilgrimages declined a little in the 18th century, as did religious practice in general. Rulers such as Joseph II, influenced by the rationalism of the Enlightenment, suppressed shrines and forbade subjects to leave on foreign pilgrimages. However, after the anti-religious excesses of the French Revolution with its destruction of church property, people began once again to show an interest in religion and a new golden age of pilgrimage began in the middle of the 19th century and continued into the 20th century. Modern transportation, especially air transport, made access to shrines much easier than before. The mid-19th century rise of the railways resulted in a greater number of pilgrims visiting the larger shrines, but with the consequence that fewer people visited their local shrines. On the other hand, the 20th-century rise of the automobile brought the popular interest back to the local shrine.

Many of today's popular shrines are dedicated to individual saints: for example, Croagh Patrick in Ireland, and Lisieux in France. However, there is a predominance of Marian shrines, both national and international, such as Lourdes and Fatima, Lujan in Argentina, Czestochowa in Poland, Aparacida in Brazil, and Copacabana in Bolivia.

Post-Vatican II

In this post-Vatican II era, pilgrimages continue to hold their own. During the Council the symbol for the Church shifted from the Mystical Body of Christ to the Journeying Pilgrim People. Since the Council, more emphasis has been placed on pilgrimages as an opportunity to deepen spiritual life. The pilgrimage has come to represent the Church on the road to salvation.

Pilgrims seek the certainty of redemption in the midst of the uncertainties of the modern world. Through a pilgrimage they become more aware of the nature of redemption and of the Church as the communion of saints. Christ and the saints do not stand apart from the pilgrim Church but offer believers support and intercession.

Recent controversies, such as the one surrounding the apparitions at Medjugorje in Bosnia-Hercegovina, show the dilemma the Church faces in recognizing pilgrimages grounded in miracles: the need to allow the faith of the people to grow and develop in freedom, yet the fear of the possibility of a fraud that could undermine this very faith.

With the increase in international tourism over the past 25 years, the larger shrines are receiving record numbers of tourists. Lourdes, one of the largest of all, receives many tourists among its 5.5 million visitors each year. Lourdes welcomes the tourist along with the curiosity-seeker on the understanding that God offers conversion to everyone. However, many smaller shrines actively discourage curiosity-seekers as a distraction and even a hindrance to the pilgrim.

Today the Eastern Orthodox continue to have an interest in pilgrimages, and Jerusalem and the monasteries of Mt. Athos in Greece continue to draw pilgrims. With the decline of Communism in Eastern Europe and elsewhere, some old shrines are being reopened. The catacombs of Kiev are drawing increasing numbers of Ukrainian Catholics and Orthodox. Outside Shanghai, China, Catholic fishermen and peasants marched to the padlocked hilltop Shrine of Our Lady of Zose and forcibly took it back from the Communist government.

Meanwhile, in Western Europe there is a new interest among Protestants in visiting historical sites of the Reformation such as Geneva and Wittenberg. Protestants and Catholics have been co-operating in the revival of the ancient pilgrimage site of Iona. Anglicans and Catholics have been organizing pilgrimages to the Shrine of Our Lady of Walsingham. The designation of newer shrines as significant shrines cannot be predicted, but the tomb of the martyred Archbishop Romero in El Salvador, Central America, and the enormous Shrine of Our Lady of Peace in Ivory Coast, West Africa, look promising.

II. Shrines in Canadian History

Early Period

During the time of the explorers, the first Christian shrines were established in what is present-day Canada. The crosses planted by Cartier at Gaspé in 1534 and by Maisonneuve on Mount Royal in 1642 were like harbingers of the countless wayside crosses of later centuries. The missionary fervour of the Récollets and Jesuits of early 17th-century Canada reflected the vigour of the Catholic Reformation in France. The Church in early Canada was blessed with exceptional men, such as Jean Brébeuf and Bishop Laval, and formidable women, such as Marie de l'Incarnation, Jeanne Mance and Marguerite d'Youville.

Devotion to Ste. Anne was strong among the settlers, and in 1658 the first shrine was erected at Ste. Anne de Beaupré. Eventually, shrines to Ste. Anne would be built all over Canada by French settlers and the newly-baptized Indians, who developed a special liking for Ste. Anne, the grandmother of Christ. In 1675 Marguerite Bourgeoys began the Shrine of Notre-Dame-de-Bon-Secours (Our Lady of Good Help) in Montreal, and in 1690 the Church of Notre-Dame-des-Victoires (Our Lady of the Victories) in Quebec City became a shrine.

The 18th and 19th Centuries

In the early 18th century, France neglected Canada and the colony declined. With the 1759–1760 conquest by Britain, the Catholic Church in Canada entered a new period of decline. The British, although formally recognizing the Catholic Church, hoped that the French colonists would eventually become Protestant. Popular piety, including pilgrimages, almost disappeared.

By the early 19th century, however, the British became more disposed toward the Catholic Church because of its support against the invading Americans. After the fall of Napoleon in 1815, popular piety began to recover in Europe, but it was only after the rebellions in Upper and Lower Canada of 1837 and 1838 that the same kind of recovery began in Canada.

The late 19th century was the first great age of pilgrimage in Canada. With the encouragement of Bishop Bourget of Montreal, old shrines were reopened and new ones begun. Rome's proclamation of the Dogma of the Immaculate Conception in 1854 and the Lourdes apparitions of 1858 created a Marian interest that culminated in the founding of Marian shrines at Rigaud in 1874 and at Cap-de-la-Madeleine in 1888.

In 1889 the pilgrimage to Lac Ste. Anne, Alberta, began. Rising interest in devotions to the Sacred Heart of Jesus led to the creation of the shrine at Pointe-aux-Trembles, Quebec, in 1896. The development of railways and steamships brought ever-increasing numbers of pilgrims to Ste. Anne de Beaupré and Oka. At the same time, the popularity of wayside crosses in rural Quebec became so great that the bishops had to limit them. It was a common custom for people to gather at a wayside cross for evening prayers.

The 20th Century

In 1904 Brother André founded his first shrine to St. Joseph on Mount Royal. This was followed by the building of the first hermitage to St. Anthony at Lac Bouchette in 1907. Popular religious feeling was at a new high when Montreal hosted the 21st International Eucharistic Congress in 1910. Combined with the revival of Acadian national feeling, it led to the creation of the Acadian national shrine at Rogersville, New Brunswick, in 1912. During World War I, shrines to the Sacred Heart were established at Sillery and Beauvoir, both in Quebec.

In 1926 the shrine to the Canadian Martyrs was built at Midland, Ontario, providing a new reason for pilgrimage in Canada – local saints. The economic hard times of the 1930s led to the establishment of several western shrines, such as the one at Blumenfeld, Saskatchewan. Just as groups of Irish and Scottish settlers had been involved with the founding of shrines in the Atlantic Provinces, Quebec and Ontario, in the West shrines were founded by groups of Poles, Hungarians, German Rumanians, German Russians, and especially the Ukrainians, the Indians and missionaries from Quebec.

The second great period of Canadian pilgrimage occurred in the 1940s and 50s. This was a boom time in religious practice, especially after World War II. Pilgrimage fervour was fuelled by the Marian Congress in Ottawa in 1947, the Holy Year of 1950 and the Marian Year of 1954. Record numbers of pilgrims travelled to shrines all over the country, especially in Quebec. Among the new shrines founded at this time were Marylake at King City (Ontario), Notre-Dame-du-Mont-Saint-Joseph in the Gaspé and Montreal's Mary, Queen of Hearts.

Post-Vatican II

The Second Vatican Council (1962–1965) caused an abrupt shift away from popular devotions. With a greater emphasis placed on biblical studies, renewed liturgies, and pastoral and social justice concerns, pilgrimages began to wane. In Quebec the decline was accelerated by the so-called Quiet Revolution, which removed the Church from the centre of Quebec public life. During this time many of the smaller and newer shrines closed.

This was also a time, however, when Canadian shrines took part in the Vatican II renewal – reforming their liturgies, situating popular devotions in basic Christian doctrine, and doing more counselling and other pastoral work. During the 1970s it became clear that the larger shrines were not only surviving but were attracting ever larger numbers of pilgrims.

The Holy Years of 1975 and 1983 and the interest in pilgrimage shown by Pope John Paul II all contributed to a revival. Canonizations and beatifications brought new pilgrims to the tombs of Marguerite d'Youville, Brother André, Kateri Tekakwitha and others.

The Marian Year of 1987–1988 brought the erection of Marian shrines in countless parish churches across the country, the refurbishing of old shrines, and even the building of a few new sanctuaries such as those at Freshwater (Newfoundland), Cache Creek (British Columbia), and the Ukrainian Catholic National Shrine in Ottawa, which also celebrates the millennium of Christianity in Ukraine. All signs seem to indicate that we are already in a new age of pilgrimage.

Newfoundland

BELL ISLAND

Grotto of the Sacred Heart of Jesus

Bell Island is on Conception Bay, a few kilometres northwest of St. John's. Take Highway 40 from St. John's to Portugal Cove. From Portugal Cove there is a regular ferry to the island.

Bell Island's iron ore mines, once the largest in the world, were shut down in the early 1960s. As a result, one of the three Catholic parishes on the island was forced to close its doors. The Grotto of the Sacred Heart in Lance Cove commemorates that parish. There is an outdoor Stations of the Cross here arranged in the outline of a bell.

An annual Mass is celebrated in July or August.

FATHER DUFFY'S WELL PARK

Father Duffy's Well

The Well is in the middle of the Avalon Peninsula on Highway 90 beside Salmonier Nature Park.

In the 1840s Father James Duffy used to walk through this park to minister to the Irish at Holyrood. His preaching fervour often roused his people to action and once he was charged with inciting a riot. One day, having been summoned to St. John's to explain himself to the bishop, he discovered this spring along the way. Other travellers began to stop here for a rest.

Today many local people consider the Well holy and come here to pray and to collect water to bring home.

There is a picnic ground here.

FERRYLAND

Grotto of Our Lady of Fatima

Ferryland is on the east coast of the Avalon Peninsula on Highway 10, close to Renews. The name derives from the French word *forillon.*

In 1621 George Calvert, 1st Baron Baltimore, established a colony here (Avalon) but later moved it to Maryland (now in the U.S.A.).

The grotto stands on the grounds of The Downs Inn. It was blessed in 1961 and is a place for local devotion. In front of the parish church at Bay Bulls are reminders of naval battles between the French, Dutch and English – four cannons serve as pedestals for statues of Saints Patrick, Joseph, Paul and Theresa.

FLATROCK

Grotto of Our Lady of Lourdes

From St. John's take Highway 20 north for approximately 20 kilometres. The name Flatrock dates from the 17th century and refers to the flat rocks around the cove which were ideal for drying codfish.

History

To celebrate the Marian Year of 1954, the parishioners of St. Agnes Church in Pouch Cove set up a fund for a Marian shrine. That same year their parish priest, Father William Sullivan, had gone on a pilgrimage to Lourdes, France. He realized that the terrain around Flatrock would be suitable for a replica of the Lourdes grotto. The shrine was finished in 1958, the centenary of Lourdes, and dedicated by Archbishop Skinner.

On September 12, 1984, the shrine received a great deal of attention when Pope John Paul II came to bless the inshore fishing fleet in the harbour at Flatrock and stopped at the shrine to pray.

The Shrine

The shrine is on a stone outcropping and overlooks Flatrock harbour. The grotto has an altar, pulpit and open space in front for pilgrims. On both sides of the grotto is a path with a beautiful marble Way of the Cross. It rises to a terrace at the top of the rock where there is a crucifix over 3.5 metres high.

To Help You Plan Your Pilgrimage

Schedule: The Grotto is open to the public during daylight hours year round. From the last week of June to Labour Day there is Rosary and Benediction every Sunday afternoon. The Feast of Our Lady of Mount Carmel (July 16) is celebrated with an evening Rosary, Benediction and Investing with the Brown Scapular. The Feast of St. Anne and St. Joachim (July 26) is celebrated with an evening Mass and the Blessing of the Sick. The Legion of Mary from the parishes of the Archdiocese of St. John's makes an annual pilgrimage on the Sunday nearest August 15. A triduum is held August 13-15, and on the night of the Feast of the Assumption (August 15) all the local parishes take part in a candlelight procession from the parish church to the shrine, followed by a Mass, the Rosary and a blessing. On the Feast of the Triumph of the Cross (September 14) there is a Way of the Cross.

For your convenience: There is parking on the site and washrooms at St. Michael's Church. On pilgrimage days there is lunch at the nearby community centre.

For further information: St. Agnes and St. Michael's Parish, Box 10, Pouch Cove, NF A0A 3L0. ☎ (709) 335-2863; 🖷 (709) 335-8240; e-mail: fpud@nf.sympatico.ca.

Also of interest: All along the coast there are icebergs in the spring and whale watching.

FRESHWATER

Grotto of Our Lady of Lourdes

Freshwater is in the western Avalon Peninsula by Highway 100, halfway between Argentia and historic Placentia.

To celebrate the Marian Year of 1987–88, the parish of Holy Rosary decided to build a grotto for the statues of Mary and Bernadette that had been on the church grounds for decades. Tonnes of rock were blasted out of the hillside to provide a place reminiscent of the Grotto of Massabielle at Lourdes. On the Feast of the Assumption in 1988, there was a procession to the grotto, a Mass and a blessing of the shrine and of the spring that had been discovered while the rock was being excavated.

LAMALINE

Our Lady of Lourdes Grotto

Lamaline is on the Burin Peninsula. From Goobies, take Highway 210 southwest, then Highways 222, 221 and finally Highway 220.

The grotto was founded by parish priest Msgr. Eric Lawlor in the late 1940s. It is situated on Allan's Island; a causeway goes to the island.

To Help You Plan Your Pilgrimage

Schedule: This is a shrine of local pilgrimage. Pilgrimage day is the Feast of the Assumption (August 15) but not necessarily every year.

For further information: St. Joseph's Parish, P.O. Box 68, Lamaline, Placentia Bay, NF A0E 2C0.

Also of interest: Not far away are the Grand Banks. There is a ferry to the French islands of St. Pierre and Miquelon.

MARYSTOWN

Shrine of Marymount

Marystown is on fiord-like Mortier Bay on the Burin Peninsula in southeastern Newfoundland. From the Trans-Canada Highway at Goobies, take Highway 210.

On top of a hill overlooking Marystown is a large pillar with a beautiful statue of Our Lady of the World. It is visible from all over the town, especially at night, when it is lit. The shrine was constructed in 1976 in memory of the Fitzpatrick family and in thanksgiving for a general improvement in employment in the community.

Marian devotions are held here. On the Feast of the Assumption (August 15) there is a local pilgrimage.

Accommodations and restaurants are available in the town.

MOUNT CARMEL

Grotto of Our Lady of Mount Carmel

Mount Carmel is near the centre of the Avalon Peninsula. Take Highway 90 and turn at Salmonier. The grotto is on a spur road beyond St. Catherine's and overlooks the scenic Salmonier Arm.

The Church of Mount Carmel was first blessed in 1883. At that time a wooden statue of Our Lady of Mount Carmel, a gift from Pope Leo XIII, was placed above the tower of the church.

In the early 1900s a windstorm blew the statue off its perch but it was only slightly damaged. It soon became known as a miraculous statue among the local people and it was placed in the church porch and later in a nearby garden.

In 1988 the parishioners responded to Pope John Paul's invitation to celebrate the Marian Year and built a grotto in which they placed the old statue.

Father Duffy's Well is not far away. (See separate entry.)

OUTER COVE

St. Ann's Grotto

Outer Cove is just north of St. John's on the Atlantic Ocean. The grotto is near the Church of St. Francis of Assisi.

There had always been a strong devotion to St. Ann in this parish and the grotto was erected in the early 1950s by the parish priest, Father Robert St. John.

RENEWS

Grotto of Our Lady of Lourdes

Renews is on the Avalon Peninsula on the Atlantic Ocean. It is 80 kilometres south of St. John's on Highway 10.

History

For most of the 17th and 18th centuries, the British government discouraged settlement in Newfoundland, especially settlement by Roman Catholics. Irish Catholics, fleeing the penal laws in Ireland, soon discovered that there were also penal laws in Newfoundland that exacted special taxes of them and that also forbade the celebration of Mass. Priests were outlawed but some came over disguised as fishermen. They moved among the people, celebrating secret Masses at places that were called Mass rocks. The grotto at Renews is built on Midnight Rock, one of those old Mass rocks.

The Shrine

The Grotto of Our Lady of Lourdes was established in 1927 by parish priest Father Charles McCarthy, who was originally from Ireland. The grotto contains the marble votive statue, an altar and pulpit, and a piece of the rock of the original grotto at Lourdes, France. A path to the right side of the grotto leads through a wooded area with a Stations of the Cross.

To Help You Plan Your Pilgrimage

Schedule: The grotto is next to the church of the Holy Apostles and is accessible at all times in all seasons. The Feast of the Assumption (August 15) is celebrated with an outdoor Mass and the Blessing of the Sick.

For your convenience: Both grotto and church are accessible to the handicapped. There are accommodations at Cappahayden, Aquafont and Renews.

For further information: Phillippa Dunne ☎ (709) 363-2345; 🖳 (709) 363-2132; e-mail: cpdunne@nf.sympatico.ca.

Also of interest: The Grotto at Ferryland is not far away. (See separate entry.)

SEARSTON

Grotto of St. Theresa

Searston is about 40 kilometres northwest of Port aux Basques. Take the Trans-Canada Highway and Highway 407. The grotto is near the church.

There is also a Stations of the Cross and a Rosary made of rose bushes.

ST. JOHN'S

Shrine of Our Lady of Fatima

This tiny shrine is in the west transept of the historic Basilica of St. John the Baptist.

The Fatima group of statues was donated by Portuguese fishermen in 1955 in recognition of the five centuries the Portuguese have been coming to fish on the Grand Banks of Newfoundland. Thousands of Portuguese fishermen marched from the dock to the basilica carrying the statues.

Nova Scotia

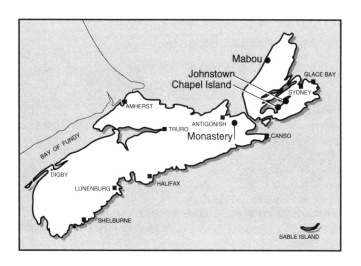

Mabou
Johnstown
Chapel Island
GLACE BAY
SYDNEY
AMHERST
ANTIGONISH
TRURO
Monastery
CANSO
BAY OF FUNDY
DIGBY
LUNENBURG
HALIFAX
SHELBURNE
SABLE ISLAND

CHAPEL ISLAND

Chapel of St. Ann

The community of Chapel Island is in southwestern Cape Breton Island. From Port Hawkesbury, take Highway 4 about 60 kilometres. The shrine is on an island on Bras d'Or Lake just north of the community.

This is the Holy Land of the Micmac. The mission was founded here on Pentecost Sunday in 1629.

To Help You Plan Your Pilgrimage

Schedule: The Chapel is open from early May to November. The big celebration is the Feast of St. Anne (the last Sunday in July). The weekend begins on Thursday evening with Reconciliation and Mass. On Friday and Saturday there are evening Masses. Saturday is Youth Day. On Sunday there is a Mass, a procession around a rock where the first sermon was preached in 1629, and then the blessing of the water from Ste. Anne de Beaupré. There is a talk by the grand chief and the grand council. The day ends with a procession back to the Chapel of St. Ann and an exposition of the relic of St. Ann. On Monday there is a morning Mass and Stations of the Cross. On Pentecost Sunday there is a special Mass to commemorate the founding of the shrine.

For your convenience: On pilgrimage days there are many fishing boats available to take you to the island. Everything is accessible to the handicapped. There is camping on the island but no electricity.

For further information: St. Peter's Parish, P.O. Box 130, St. Peter's, NS B0E 3B0. ☎ and 🖳 (902) 535-2053; e-mail: st.peters@ns.sympatico.ca.

Also of interest: The shrine at Johnstown is to the east. (See separate entry.)

JOHNSTOWN

Shrine of Our Lady of Guadalupe

Johnstown is on the south side of Cape Breton Island. From Port Hawkesbury, take Highway 4 east about 70 kilometres.

The shrine, the only one to Our Lady of Guadalupe in Canada, is situated next to Sacred Heart Church on a hill overlooking Bras d'Or Lake. It consists of a 10-metre-high arched stand containing an altar and a ceramic plaque of Our Lady of Guadalupe. In front are statues of Aztec Juan Diego and his bishop. All were imported from Mexico.

To Help You Plan Your Pilgrimage

Schedule: The shrine, which is outdoors, is open all year long, and the church is always open. Pilgrimage day is the Sunday closest to July 12. On that day the Micmac and other people from the surrounding parishes come for an afternoon Mass. The Feast of Our Lady of Guadalupe (December 12) is celebrated with a special Mass in the church and a procession to the shrine for devotions.

For your convenience: There are washrooms and parking at the shrine. In the sacristy of the church is a tiny art gallery consisting of 12 paintings of Our Lady of Guadalupe in an aboriginal style by Brazilian artist Claudio Pastro.

Every year the shrine organizes a pilgrimage to the Shrine of Our Lady of Guadalupe in Mexico.

For further information: St. Mary's Parish, 7215 East Bay Highway, Big Pond, NS B1J 1V2. ☎ (902) 828-2317; e-mail: mjgillis@ns.sympatico.ca; web site: www.randburg.com/ca/fiddles.html.

Also of interest: Not far away is Big Pond with an annual Scottish concert and Rita MacNeil's teahouse. Don't miss historic Fort Louisbourg.

MABOU

Our Mother of Sorrows Pioneer Shrine

Mabou is on the northwest coast of Cape Breton Island and is about 60 kilometres from the Canso Causeway. Take Route 19.

History

The majority of the Catholics of Cape Breton Island are of highland Scottish descent. They came here in the late 18th and early 19th centuries because of the religious persecution and the systematic land enclosures in the highlands of Scotland. At Mabou they built their first tiny place of worship in 1800 and, in 1899, the present St. Mary's Church with its landmark spire.

In 1927 a local craftsman and carpenter, Thomas Burke, was asked to build a memorial chapel on the site of the original pioneer church. Used only occasionally, the little church fell into disuse by 1967. It was offered to the Brothers of Our Lady, who arranged to move it into Mabou, restore it and set it up as a Shrine to Our Mother of Sorrows.

The Shrine

The shrine sits on a green knoll on the side of the road. It is a wayside shrine with a picturesque exterior and a neon cross on the steeple. The interior is almost like a miniature cathedral with its natural finish woodwork. There is no altar inside. In its place is a shrine of the *Pietà*.

To Help You Plan Your Pilgrimage

Schedule: The shrine is open all year round, 24 hours a day. There are Masses at St. Mary's Church just across the bridge. Every week from May to October there is a group rosary (1-hour duration). There is an annual celebration on the second Sunday in September, with a continuous rosary from 11 a.m. to 4 p.m. and Peace Day Mass at 4 p.m.

For your convenience: The shrine has parking and a picnic area and there is a hostel next door. There are restaurants at Mabou and Inverness. In Mabou there is a hotel and several bed-and-breakfast places. There are motels at both Port Hood and Inverness.

For further information: Our Mother of Sorrows Pioneer Shrine, Mabou, NS B0E 1X0. ☎ (902) 945-2221. Web site: www.maboushrine.cjb.net.

Also of interest: The Pioneers' Cemetery at Indian Point has a memorial cairn. St. Joseph's Church at Glencoe Mills was built by Scottish settlers and has an unusual bell-tower.

MONASTERY

Our Lady of Grace Shrine

Monastery is about 35 kilometres east of Antigonish, close to the Trans-Canada Highway. The shrine is on the grounds of the Monastery of St. Augustine.

History

In 1825 this monastery was founded by Trappist monks from France, the first Trappist monastery in North America. Two fires in the 1890s put an end to its prosperity, destroying both the monastery and the farm buildings. The present monastery was built in 1892, but in 1900 the monks moved to Rhode Island, U.S.A. In 1903 another group of Trappists, fleeing persecution in France, arrived and took over the monastery. They returned to France in 1919 and were replaced in 1938 by the present Augustinian Order.

The Shrine

The shrine was established in 1952 by Father Leo Ebert, who had gained experience at the Marylake Shrine in King City, Ontario. The devotion of the local people, however, goes back to the discovery of the hidden spring in the woods by the third Trappist Prior in the late 19th century. People began to report cures and the water became known as the Holy Spring. The shrine is located 1.5 kilometres from the monastery and may be reached by a path through the woods.

Along the path is a Stations of the Cross consisting of metal reliefs on white marble plaques attached to crosses. In a clearing is the Holy Spring with the statue of Our Lady of Grace. To the left are stairs leading to a crucifix that is 5 metres high and has a roof over it. Further on is a grotto with a *Pietà*. There is also a chapel to St. Ann and a shrine to St. Joseph.

The Chapel

St. Augustine's Chapel was built in 1960 in the design of New York architect Michael Segalas. The interior is beautifully decorated. In the sanctuary the altar table is of white marble with a wooden baldachino above it in the shape of a crown of thorns.

The Blessed Sacrament altar has ceramic-tile mosaics by American Jean Nison, a tabernacle by German goldsmith Max Bessler, and a crucifix by Swiss artist Emil Thomann. There are five side chapels and countless works of art, including 16 paintings of Augustinian saints by Earl Neiman.

In the former porterhouse of the monastery is a small museum of Trappist and Augustinian history, and a nature collection that includes minerals and fossils. There is also a small gallery of paintings by Father Luke Schrepfter, OSA.

To Help You Plan Your Pilgrimage
Schedule: The shrine is open year round for private prayer. The Rosary and Benediction are prayed every Sunday afternoon from May to October at the chapel. The Feast of St. Anne (the Sunday after July 25) is celebrated with Rosary, Benediction and a sermon in the chapel, followed by a procession to the shrine.

For your convenience: There is parking by the chapel and washrooms in the retreat house. Accommodations and restaurants are available in Antigonish and Port Hawkesbury.

For further information: The Prior, St. Augustine's Monastery, Monastery, NS B0H 1W0. ☎ and 🖳 (902) 232-2214; e-mail: monksofstmaron@ns.sympatico.ca.

Also of interest: St. Ninian's Cathedral in Antigonish contains paintings by Canadian artist Ozias Leduc.

Prince Edward Island

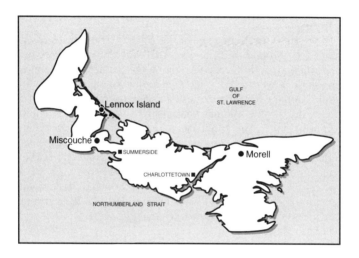

GULF
OF
ST. LAWRENCE

Lennox Island

Miscouche ●

■ SUMMERSIDE

● Morell

CHARLOTTETOWN ■

NORTHUMBERLAND STRAIT

LENNOX ISLAND

Shrine of St. Ann

Lennox Island is a Micmac reserve off the north shore of western Prince Edward Island. Take Highway 2 west to Mount Pleasant. Just past Mount Pleasant take Highway 133. At the crossroads take Route 12 northwest a few kilometres to Route 163, which will take you on to Lennox Island.

History

In 1610 the high chief of the Micmac, Membertou, was baptized. Around 1620 a concordat was drawn up between the Micmac and the papacy, giving the district chiefs almost the same powers as the priests, including the right to teach the faith. After the British conquest of Canada and the expulsion of the Acadians, the Micmac were responsible for the survival of Catholicism in the Maritime region. Every Sunday twelve Micmac – six elders carrying large crosses and six youths carrying small crosses – led their people in a procession. They celebrated the Mass except for the Consecration.

From the earliest times the Micmac adopted St. Ann, the grandmother of Christ, as their patroness, partly because of their great respect for grandmothers. The pilgrimage to St. Ann has a very long history.

The Shrine

The wooden Church of St. Ann is a typical Maritime rural church on the outside with its single spire and fish-scale shingles. The statue of St. Ann carrying the child Mary is on the right-hand altar and there is a reliquary stand here. On the altar on the left side of the church is a tabernacle in the shape of a teepee. High above it on the wall is a 200-year-old wooden processional cross once carried by an elder during the weekly liturgy.

To Help You Plan Your Pilgrimage

Schedule: There is a pilgrimage on the Feast of St. Ann (celebrated on the Sunday after July 26). A triduum precedes it. On Sunday there is a morning Mass in front of the St. Ann statue in the field opposite the church. This is followed by a healing service and occasionally a blessing of the fishing fleet.

For your convenience: Lunch is served in the nearby hall. There is a handicrafts store on the reserve with material from many tribes.

MISCOUCHE

Calvary

Miscouche is on Highway 2 west of Summerside in the Acadian region of western Prince Edward Island.

During the deportation of the Acadians in the 1750s and 60s, some Acadians fled to the woods and managed to survive. Some of the deportees later returned to the region.

The Calvary is in the cemetery behind the twin-spired Church of St. John the Baptist. There is an Acadian pioneer monument here too, and a Lourdes grotto in front of the former convent.

MORELL

Grotto of the Little Flower

Morell is on Highway 2 about 40 kilometres northeast of Charlottetown. The grotto is on Little Flower Avenue, next to the Church of St. Theresa.

The grotto was built in 1983 on the site of the original parish church. Nearby is a modern bell-tower with a carillon.

New Brunswick

QUÉBEC

CHALEUR BAY

GULF OF
ST. LAWRENCE

Caraquet

Sheila ● Tracadie

● Ste-Anne-de-Madawaska

Burnt Church

NORTHUMBERLAND STRAIT

Saint-Louis-de-Kent

Howard ●

UNITED STATES OF AMERICA

N

Rogersville

Cap-Pelé ●

MONCTON ■

NOVA SCOTIA

● Skiff Lake

SAINT JOHN

BAY OF FUNDY

BURNT CHURCH

St. Ann's Shrine

Burnt Church is in northeastern New Brunswick, about 30 kilometres northeast of Chatham.

To Help You Plan Your Pilgrimage

Schedule: The annual pilgrimage day is the Feast of St. Ann (the Sunday closest to July 26). There is a Mass, a procession and Blessing of the Sick.

For your convenience: Parking is available and food is served at the nearby school.

For further information: St. Ann Parish, R.R. #1, Lagaceville, NB E0C 1K0.

Also of interest: The Shrine to St. Joseph at Tracadie is to the northeast. (See separate entry.)

CAP-PELÉ

Calvary

Cap-Pelé is on Highway 15 east of Shediac. At the cross-roads is a statue of an angel. In the cemetery of the Parish of St. Teresa of Avila is a beautiful Calvary group.

Another Calvary is located at nearby Port Elgin.

CARAQUET

Shrine of Ste. Anne du Bocage

Caraquet is northeast of Bathurst by Highway 11, and north-east of Chatham by Highway 11. The shrine is on St-Pierre Street, about 3 kilometres from the Church of St-Pierre-aux-Liens. The place is quiet and peaceful and, as the name *bocage* suggests, surrounded by a pleasant landscape of grass and trees, with the sea nearby.

History

While this shrine honours Ste. Anne, the mother of Mary, it also commemorates the return of the first Acadians after their deportation. In 1755, having seized the Acadian region from France four decades earlier, the British decided that the Acadians were untrustworthy. The British deported 10,000 Acadians to places all over the British Empire and to France. Later some of the Acadians, including the founders of Caraquet, were able to return. On July 22, 1857, a ship was wrecked near Caraquet and 56 people drowned. The survivors walked from the quay of Caraquet to the chapel to pray to Ste. Anne. From that time on, it was known as a Shrine of Ste. Anne.

The Shrine

At the entrance to the shrine grounds is a monument with a plaque commemorating the return in 1756 of Acadian Alexis Landry. There are several other monuments on the grounds.

The chapel has a bell-tower. The walls of the back of the chapel can be removed to provide a sanctuary for outdoor celebrations. In the chapel is the statue of Ste. Anne, the patron of sailors and fishermen. In the *bocage* is a Grotto to Our Lady of the Assumption, a Way of the Cross and a Way of the Rosary. A stairway descends to the water's edge, where there is a quay and a stone structure that holds the spring that served the founders of Caraquet around 1760.

To Help You Plan Your Pilgrimage

Schedule: The shrine is open during the day, year round. During the novena preceding the Feast of Ste. Anne (July 26), there are daily Masses and devotions. On the feast day itself there are several Masses and a Blessing of the Sick in the afternoon. Some local parishes organize pilgrimages on foot on this day. On the Sunday following the Feast of Ste. Anne, the Mass of the Fishermen is celebrated. The Feast of the Assumption (August 15) is the Acadian National Day. There is a Solemn Mass celebrated in the morning.

For your convenience: Parking and washrooms are available on the grounds. The shrine is accessible to the handicapped. There are picnic tables on the grounds and a religious articles stand. There are hotels, motels and restaurants in Caraquet.

For further information: Parish of Caraquet, P.O. Box 360, Caraquet, NB E0B 1K0. ☎ (506) 727-3212; 📠 (506) 727-7325.

Also of interest: Caraquet is the centre of Acadian culture. At the beginning of August, the Bishop of Bathurst blesses the flag-bedecked fishing fleet and the Caraquet Festival of Acadian music and culture begins. Grand-Anse, to the northwest, features the Pope's Museum, housing a gallery of portraits of popes, a model of St. Peter's in Rome and a general history of Catholicism.

HOWARD

Shrine of Our Lady of Mount Carmel

Howard is on the Southwest Miramichi River close to the geographical centre of New Brunswick. From Fredericton take Highway 8 and turn right at Upper Blackville.

Mount Carmel

Mount Carmel, overlooking Haifa in Israel, was the site of several Marian shrines established by hermits living there. From some of these hermits the Carmelite Order developed. In 1251 in Cambridge, England, Carmelite St. Simon Stock reported a vision in which the Virgin of Mount Carmel gave him the brown scapular (symbolizing the burden of Christ's cross) to wear. This is commemorated in the Feast of Our Lady of Mount Carmel.

The mission Church of Our Lady of Mount Carmel was founded and built by Irish settlers in Howard in 1836. In the 1987–88 Marian Year, the Howard shrine became diocesan.

To Help You Plan Your Pilgrimage

Schedule: Pilgrimage day is the Feast of Our Lady of Mount Carmel (the Sunday closest to July 16). There is a pavilion for outdoor Masses on the church grounds.

ROGERSVILLE

National Monument of Our Lady of the Assumption

Rogersville is near the southern border between Northumberland and Kent counties in eastern New Brunswick. From Moncton take Highway 126 north.

History

The Shrine of Our Lady of the Assumption is the national monument of the Acadians in Canada. It was founded by Msgr. Marcel François Richard, the catalyst for the Acadian renaissance of the late 19th and early 20th centuries.

Msgr. Richard had been given an 8-foot statue of the Virgin by organizers of the 1910 International Eucharistic Congress in Montreal. It became the centrepiece of the monument, which was completed in 1912. When Msgr. Richard died in 1915 his tomb was placed inside the shrine. In 1969 the shrine burned but was replaced by a new one in 1972. The pilgrimage became diocesan in 1975.

The Shrine

The shrine is of unusual design – it is eight-sided and three stories high. The entrance to the shrine is through a pointed archway and is flanked by fieldstone stands holding statues of angels. These were erected during the 1955 bicentenary of the deportation of the Acadians. Over the entrance is a statue of Our Lady of the Assumption. Inside is an altar, a large mosaic of the Assumption of the Virgin Mary and the tomb of Msgr. Richard.

On the grounds are several monuments, some of them gifts from Acadians in the U.S.A. On the tree-lined walk is the statue of Msgr. Richard. It has a fieldstone cairn beneath it with a bas-relief plaque illustrating Pope Pius X presenting Msgr. Richard with a chalice in recognition of the Acadians as a people. There is also a Grotto of Our Lady of Lourdes, a Way of the Cross and a Grotto of Our Lady of Fatima.

To Help You Plan Your Pilgrimage

Schedule: The grounds are open from June 1 to September 30. The Feast of the Assumption (August 15) is the Acadian National Day. There is a novena from August 6 to 14 and each day of the novena is set aside for pilgrims from specific parishes. One day of the novena is for English-speaking pilgrims, while another is for families. On the feast day, in the morning there is the Exposition of the Blessed Sacrament and the Rosary at the shrine, and also a Mass at the Foyer Assomption. In the afternoon, there is a Marian Hour at the parish church, a gathering of the young at the arch, a celebration for the young, and confessions in the church. In the evening there is a Mass in the shrine and a candlelight procession. This is followed by a program of Acadian music.

For your convenience: There is parking on the grounds. The shrine is accessible to the handicapped. There are washrooms on the grounds and a religious articles shop. There are motels about 2 kilometres from the shrine. There are several restaurants and a place for picnicking in the village.

For further information: National Monument, Saint-François-de-Sales Parish, P.O. Box 75, Rogersville, NB E0A 2T0. ☎ (506) 775-2201.

Also of interest: There is a Trappist Monastery and a Trappistine Convent at Rogersville. The monks have room for retreatants. Richibucto has the delightful round Church of St. Aloysius Gonzaga, with a concrete roof shaped like a fluted shell and abstract stained glass windows. Not far from Richibucto is Indian Island Reservation with a Micmac church in the shape of a teepee dedicated to Kateri Tekakwitha. The Church of Ste-Anne-de-Kent is notable for a series of 48 paintings by Edward Gautreau. (See next entry.)

SAINT-LOUIS-DE-KENT

Grotto of Our Lady of Lourdes and Calvary

Saint-Louis-de-Kent is on Highway 134, not far from the Trans-Canada Highway and just outside Kouchibouguac National Park. The Lourdes Grotto is right on the bank of the Kouchibouquasis River.

The grotto was constructed around 1878 by Acadian nationalist Msgr. Richard, who was born here. The village also has an outdoor Calvary set up in 1881 and a cairn to Msgr. Richard.

The shrine at Rogersville is not far away. (See separate entry.)

SAINTE-ANNE-DE-MADAWASKA

Shrine of Ste-Anne-de-Madawaska

Sainte-Anne-de-Madawaska is in the northwestern part of the province, on the Trans-Canada Highway about 35 kilometres southeast of Edmundston.

In the 19th century, when the boundary between American and British territories was being decided, this region was known as the Republic of Madawaska. There was no contact between the proud local Acadians and any central government.

The Shrine

The shrine is in the Church of Ste-Anne on a hill facing the Saint John River. Built in 1923 of local fieldstone, the church is in the Romanesque style with two baroque-looking bell-towers. Inside the church the statue of Ste-Anne is in the left transept. There is also a large fresco by Italian painter Mario Mauro showing Ste-Anne being crowned by angels as she stands with Mary and a group of devotees in a landscape that includes the present church. The Stations of the Cross were carved by Claude Thériault.

To Help You Plan Your Pilgrimage

Schedule: The shrine is open all year round, with daily Masses and reconciliation available. The Feast of Ste-Anne (July 26) is preceded by a novena (July 17-26), during which there is a pilgrimage for the handicapped. The Rosary is prayed every evening of the novena. There is a procession at the closing of the novena. Occasionally there is the Blessing of the Sick. On the afternoon of the Feast of Ste-Anne, there is a Mass for the sick followed by benediction.

For your convenience: The shrine is fully equipped for the handicapped and there is plenty of parking. There are washrooms at the church. During the novena there is a religious articles stand at the shrine. There are a motel and a restaurant about 3 kilometres from the shrine. There are also accommodations at Edmundston and Saint-Léonard.

For further information: Sainte-Anne-de-Madawaska Shrine, P.O. Box 460, NB E0L 1G0.

Also of interest: In Edmundston is the Romanesque Cathedral of the Immaculate Conception. The Church of Notre-Dame-des-Sept-Douleurs (Our Lady of the Seven Sorrows) has an interesting Stations of the Cross by artist Claude Roussel. The Saint John River Valley is one of the most scenic drives in Canada.

SHEILA

Shrine of Notre-Dame-de-La-Salette

The community of Sheila is just south of Tracadie on Highway 11.

This is a beach area and the tiny Shrine of Notre-Dame-de-La-Salette has an outdoor Mass for tourists every Sunday during the summer months.

SKIFF LAKE

Shrine of St. Francis of Assisi

Skiff Lake is in the southwestern part of New Brunswick, not far from the Saint John River. From Fredericton take Highway 2. At the Canterbury Exit near Meductic take Route 122 to the town of Canterbury, where signs to the shrine are posted. It is 10 kilometres along Route 122 to the Upper Skiff Lake Road and 4 kilometres along that road to the shrine.

History

The Chapel of St. Joseph at Skiff Lake was built by Irish immigrants in 1865, but the Shrine of St. Francis of Assisi was dedicated only in 1923 to commemorate the 17th-century Franciscan missionaries to this part of the Saint John River Valley.

The Shrine

Today the shrine sits on a road that is a remnant of the old portage route or Missionary Trail that the Franciscans used to reach the Indians along the St. Croix River. St. Francis' love of nature is reflected in the shrine setting – an area of woods, hills and lakes. The chapel, with its woodwork carved with shamrocks, is used for prayer and private devotions. Liturgies are celebrated in the open and it never rains on pilgrimage day, so the tradition goes.

To Help You Plan Your Pilgrimage

Schedule: The shrine is accessible year round; pilgrimage day is the second Sunday of August. There is a Mass at 11 a.m. and the Sacrament of Anointing at 2 p.m. Bring a hat, sunscreen, umbrella and water for sun exposure. The Blessed Sacrament and the relics of St. Francis and St. Clare are displayed in the chapel for private devotion.

For your convenience: There are some benches on the grounds, but bring a lawn chair and a picnic lunch. There are washrooms and a canteen on the grounds. There are a restaurant and a motel nearby. There are campgrounds at Nackawic and at Woodstock.

For further information: St. Francis Shrine, P.O. Box 670, Nackawic, NB E0H 1P0. ☎ (506) 575-2177; 🖷 (506) 575-0009; e-mail: simonjud@nb.sympatico.ca; web site: www.megspace.com/religion/simonjude/stssimon.htm.

Also of interest: The Church of St. Thomas in Canterbury is over a century old. A monument to the earliest Catholic chapel of the region (1717, Fort Meductic) is on Highway 2 near Meductic.

TRACADIE

Shrine of St. Joseph

Tracadie is on a peninsula between the Bay of Chaleur and the Gulf of St. Lawrence in northeastern New Brunswick. It can be reached from both Bathurst and Chatham by Highway 11.

History

The village of Tracadie was founded by Acadians who managed to return to Acadia after they had been deported by the British government in 1755. The Parish of St. Jean Baptiste was founded in 1842 and the present stone Gothic church dates from 1926.

The Shrine

The Shrine of St. Joseph is in the woods near the parish church. It was founded in 1955 by Father Pierre Trudel and built in the style of the Acadian memorial chapel at Grand Pré, Nova Scotia. Inside are some interesting stained glass windows and a statue of St. Joseph. On the facade is an open porch for the celebration of outdoor Masses. On the grounds are a Way of the Cross, a Way of the Rosary and a fountain to St. Joseph.

To Help You Plan Your Pilgrimage

Schedule: The shrine is open from June to September. The last three days of July are pilgrimage days. At that time there is a triduum to St. Joseph with daily evening Masses as well as devotions and Blessing of the Sick.

For your convenience: There is plenty of parking available. There are washrooms and there is a religious articles shop. The grounds are accessible to the handicapped. There are accommodations and restaurants at Tracadie and vicinity.

Also of interest: The Acadian fishing village on the Island of Lamèque has the Church of Ste-Cécile, whose whole interior is covered in bright designs painted on silk. Every summer the Lamèque Baroque Music Festival is held in the church. The shrines at Caraquet and Sheila are not far away. (See separate entries.)

Quebec

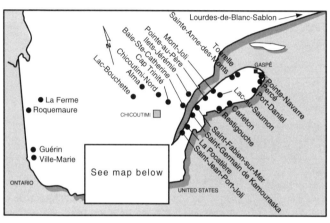

Lourdes-de-Blanc-Sablon

Sainte-Anne-des-Monts
Mont-Joli
Pointe-au-Père
Îlets-Jérémie
Baie-Ste-Catherine
Chicoutimi-Nord
Cap Trinité
Alma
Lac-Bouchette
Torelle
GASPÉ
Pointe-Navarre
Percé
Port-Daniel
Lac-au-Saumon
Carleton
Restigouche
CHICOUTIMI
Saint-Fabien-sur-Mer
Saint-Germain de
La Pocatière
Saint-Jean-Port-Joli
Kamouraska

La Ferme
Roquemaure

Guérin
Ville-Marie

See map below

ONTARIO
UNITED STATES

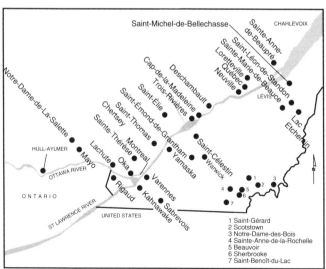

Saint-Michel-de-Bellechasse
CHARLEVOIX
Sainte-Anne-de-Beaupré
Saint-Léon-de-Standon
Sainte-Marie-de-Beauce
Loretteville
Québec
Neuville
LÉVIS
Cap-de-la-Madeleine
Deschambault
Trois-Rivières
Saint-Élie
Saint-Émond-de-Grantham
Saint-Thomas
Chertsey
Montréal
Notre-Dame-de-La-Salette
Sainte-Thérèse
Lac
Etchemin
Saint-Célestin
Warwick
HULL-AYLMER
Mayo
Lachute
Oka
Yamaska
OTTAWA RIVER
Varennes
Rigaud
Kahnawake
Sabrevois
ONTARIO
ST LAWRENCE RIVER
UNITED STATES

1 Saint-Gérard
2 Scotstown
3 Notre-Dame-des-Bois
4 Sainte-Anne-de-la-Rochelle
5 Beauvoir
6 Sherbrooke
7 Saint-Benoît-du-Lac

ALMA

Chapel of Ste. Anne

Alma is about 60 kilometres northwest of Chicoutimi. Take Highway 170 west and Highway 169 north. The little wooden Chapel of Ste. Anne is on the Island of Ste. Anne.

The chapel was built by François Gagné in 1917 on his own island in fulfilment of a vow. Today it is in the city-owned Parc Ste-Anne (Ste. Anne Park). Every year on the Feast of Ste. Anne (July 26) there is a local pilgrimage with an outdoor Mass on the steps of the chapel.

Also of interest: When in Alma do not fail to see the Church of St. Joseph, with its decorated interior and large series of stained glass windows. The Church of St. Pierre, built in the modern style, is also worth a visit.

BAIE-STE-CATHERINE

Shrine of Notre-Dame-de-l'Espace

Baie-Ste-Catherine is near the mouth of the Saguenay River, almost opposite Tadoussac. On a hill near the parish church is the small Shrine of Notre-Dame-de-l'Espace. Pilgrimage day is on a Sunday in May.

At Tadoussac is the old chapel built in 1747 with a bell from the earlier Jesuit church of 1641.

BEAUVOIR

Shrine of the Sacred Heart

Beauvoir is situated in the wooded hills on the edge of Sherbrooke in the Eastern Townships. From Sherbrooke take Highway 10-55 toward Drummondville, then Exit 143 toward Thetford. After 3 kilometres take Exit 146 and turn left onto Boulevard St-Francois. Turn left again onto Chemin de Beauvoir to the hill called Beauvoir or Beau à voir (beautiful to see).

The Sacred Heart

In the devotion to the Sacred Heart, the heart of Jesus is honoured as a symbol of Christ's love for the human race. The devotion was already known for centuries when, in the 1670s, St. Margaret Mary Alacoque received apparitions of Jesus of the Sacred Heart and was commissioned to spread the devotion. In 1856 Pope Pius IX extended the observance of the Feast of the Sacred Heart to the entire Church.

The Shrine

The shrine was founded by Father Laporte and Assumptionist Father Staub in 1917, the same year as Canadian Montmartre. Near the entrance to the grounds is the Villa Notre-Dame Residence with a large statue of the Sacred Heart of Jesus standing on a globe. Nearby is the old chapel made of local fieldstone with a little belfry on the gable.

Next to the chapel is the shrine church with a white tower and steeple that are reminiscent of the New England colonial style. The cross with the weathervane on top reminds us that this is Quebec. Inside the chapel is a statue of Jesus of the Sacred Heart. Most liturgies are held in this church, though some are held outdoors.

To get to the outdoor sanctuary in the woods, take the path to the left of the old chapel. Along the path is a statue of Mary. In front of the outdoor sanctuary are enough pews to seat nearly 1,600 people. The whole atmosphere here is one of quiet and tranquility.

Around the sanctuary is a beautiful Way of the Cross with a fine stone Calvary group sculpted by Montreal artist Joseph Guardo. Interestingly enough the Calvary is also part of an unusual Gospel Walk, a pathway of eight sculptured groups on the life of Christ by Guardo. From the Gospel Walk a stairway is necessary to reach the Calvary at the level of the Way of the Cross and so there is a *Scala Sancta* here. Also near the Calvary is a Grotto of Our Lady of Lourdes.

To Help You Plan Your Pilgrimage

Schedule: The grounds are open until 8:30 or 9:00 p.m. from the first Sunday in May to the last Sunday of October. The Feast of the Sacred Heart of Jesus is a moveable feast – the Friday following the second Sunday after Pentecost (which usually falls in June). The following Sunday is celebrated as the Solemnity of the Sacred Heart; a novena precedes or follows the Solemnity. The Feast of the Assumption (August 15) is especially important and there is a triduum preceding it. Write for further information on these and other activities.

For your convenience: The shrine is fully equipped for the handicapped. Villa Notre-Dame offers reasonable rates, but reservations must be made early. For reservations, write: 165, Rang #1, Stoke, QC J0B 3G0. ☎ (819) 846-2310. There are plenty of hotels and motels in Sherbrooke. The shrine has a cafeteria and a picnic area.

For further information: Director, Beauvoir Shrine, 169 Beauvoir Road, Bromptonville, QC J0B 1H0. ☎ (819) 569-2535; 🖳 (819) 566-6665; e-mail: beauvoir@abacom.com; web site: www.sanctuairedebeauvoir.qc.ca. In co-operation with Sillery's Canadian Montmartre, the shrine at Beauvoir produces a monthly review, *L'Appel du Sacré-Coeur*.

Also of interest: Sherbrooke's Cathedral of St. Michael, the Mother Léonie Centre and the Shrine of Our Mother of Perpetual Help are worth visiting.

CAP TRINITÉ

Statue of Notre-Dame-du-Saguenay

The nearest town to Cap Trinité is Rivière Éternité, which is about 60 kilometres southeast of Chicoutimi by way of Highways 372 and 170. From Rivière Éternité, it is about 10 kilometres north to Cap Trinité.

History

One winter day around 1870, Charles-Napoléon Robitaille, a travelling bookseller, was crossing the Saguenay River when the ice gave way beneath him. He made a vow to the Virgin that if he survived he would erect a statue to her. He did survive and immediately began to organize a public subscription, with the approval of the Bishop of Chicoutimi. Newspapers took up the cause and soon Robitaille was able to talk to sculptor Louis Jobin. Jobin produced a statue of Our Lady of Lourdes made of wood covered in lead and then painted. Over 8 metres high, it sits on a platform 200 metres up the side of the cliff.

To Help You Plan Your Pilgrimage

Schedule: Since the 1981 celebration of the 100th anniversary of the blessing of the statue, the Parish of Notre-Dame at Rivière-Éternité has sponsored an annual pilgrimage on the second Sunday of August. This is a diocesan pilgrimage and Mass is celebrated in the morning by the Bishop of Chicoutimi. The pilgrimage closes with Marian devotions in the late afternoon.

For your convenience: Bring a lawn chair. Mass is followed by a picnic. You can bring your own food or buy food here. There is hiking and a mini-cruise.

For further information: Notre-Dame de l'Éternité Parish, 412 Principale, Rivière Éternité, QC G0V 1P0.

Also of interest: Cap Trinité is part of the Conservation Park of the Saguenay. This is fiord country and a boat cruise is a good way to see the statue. You can take the cruise from the Park or from Chicoutimi.

CAP-DE-LA-MADELEINE

Notre-Dame-du-Cap

The Shrine of Our Lady of the Cape is the third largest shrine in Canada. Situated in the town of Cap-de-la-Madeleine, just east of Trois-Rivières, it is halfway between Montreal and Quebec City. The Shrine is located on the St. Lawrence River, which allows pilgrims to come by boat.

History

Marian devotions began in 1694 with the founding of the Brotherhood of the Rosary by Father Paul Vachon, the first parish priest. After his death in 1729, the parish was without a pastor until 1844 and parish life declined.

In 1867 a new priest, Father Luc Désilets, was shocked one day to discover a pig in the church gnawing on a discarded rosary. He decided to counter the lethargy in the parish with special Rosary devotions. The devotions prospered so much that the parish church could no longer hold everyone. Désilets and the parishioners planned a new church. For two years they cut and dressed stone on the south shore of the St. Lawrence River. They finished by the fall of 1878 but could not afford to have the stone ferried across the river.

The winter proved mild and it looked as if the river would never freeze over in order to move the stone. Father Désilets asked the parishioners to pray and he vowed that if an ice bridge formed he would maintain the old church as a permanent shrine to Our Lady of the Rosary. On March 14 a wind broke up the ice blocking the mouth of the St. Maurice River and the ice pans drifted to Cap-de-la-Madeleine and formed the beginning of a bridge across the St. Lawrence River. Soon parishioners went out on the ice to pack it and pour water over it to strengthen the bridge. For the next week parishioners drove their horses and sleds loaded with stone over this bridge – 175 loads in all.

Father Désilet's promise of a permanent shrine was not realized for more than 10 years due to lack of money and also because he wanted a sign that by restoring the church he would not be simply carrying out his own wishes. In 1888 he felt he had received that sign with the arrival of Father Frédéric Janssoone, a Franciscan who had spent years helping pilgrims in Jerusalem and renewing the tradition of the Way of the Cross there.

On the day the shrine was dedicated, June 22, the first recorded miracle took place. That evening, Fathers Désilets and Frédéric accompanied a handicapped man, Pierre Lacroix, to the shrine to pray before the statue. As they were praying, all three slowly became aware that the statue's eyes, which had been sculpted downcast, were wide open as if staring straight ahead. They examined the phenomenon from several different angles and concluded that it was no illusion. The phenomenon lasted from five to ten minutes.

By the end of the year over 10,000 pilgrims had come to the shrine. In 1896 the first trainloads of pilgrims arrived and Father Frédéric began to build the first Way of the Cross. In the early part of the 20th century the shrine and its grounds were improved and the pilgrimage reached a new height of popularity in the 1940s and 50s. A new basilica designed by architect Adrien Dufresne was consecrated in 1964.

The years following the Vatican Council were a time of decline in Marian devotions all over the world, and the Cap pilgrimage was no exception. By the mid-1970s, however, the charismatic renewal was starting to make its presence known at the shrine and pilgrimages began to increase again.

Pope John Paul II, who has the habit of going on pilgrimage to the major Marian shrine of every country he visits, visited here in 1984 on his Canadian tour. Four years later, to help celebrate the Marian Year and the centenary of Our Lady of the Cape, he beatified Father Frédéric at a ceremony in Rome.

The Shrine

The first place to visit is the old shrine church itself. Built of local fieldstone, with high-pitched gables, it is the only one of its kind left in Canada. The interior is surprisingly bright. The sanctuary is in the shape of a semi-dome, painted white, with the carved decorations covered in gold leaf. There are many *ex-voto* plaques here. The statue of Our Lady of the Cape stands above the tabernacle under a wooden canopy.

The second place to visit is the basilica. Its style is totally different from the shrine church – more like a modern version of Romanesque. Essentially it consists of a large vaulted cone intersected by three transepts. By placing the pillars at the intersections between the nave and the relatively shallow transepts, the architect assured all worshippers an unobstructed view of the altar. The upper church seats almost 2,000 people and the crypt church can accommodate 1,000.

The main decoration on the inside of the basilica is a series of stained glass windows. Designed by Dutch Oblate artist Jan Tillemans, the windows are a catechism of theology and doctrine, as well as a history of the Canadian Church. Each transept end has five lancet windows on a given theme and a rose window with related symbols. For example, the first north transept has the theme of the patron saints of Canada, while the rose window contains the arms of the 10 provinces of Canada around the Madonna and Child.

The Casavant organ in the loft has 75 stops and over 5,400 pipes.

The Grounds

As a major shrine, Our Lady of the Cape has good-sized grounds. Just beside the basilica is the residence of the Oblates of Mary Immaculate, who look after the shrine. By the main entrance to the basilica is a bookstore. Close to here is the Garden of the Virgin, where the Stations of the Rosary begin.

Near the old shrine is the beautiful Bridge of the Rosaries, festooned with giant rosaries and commemorating the 1879 bridge of ice. Crossing the bridge, one finds oneself in a lightly wooded area looking out on the river. The Stations of the Cross wind through the trees past the Outdoor Pavilion toward the House of Pilgrims. The Calvary is particularly attractive and the last station is a reproduction of the tomb in the Holy Sepulchre Church in Jerusalem, complete with onion dome.

The picturesque Lake St. Mary, with a fountain and an islet that holds the statue of the Virgin, is the location for candlelight processions in the evenings.

To Help You Plan Your Pilgrimage

Schedule: The shrine is always open, but the season for group pilgrimages runs from May 1 to October 31. The Feast of the Assumption (August 15) is celebrated and there is a novena that precedes it. Please write for further information on pilgrimages for the blind, the deaf, the sick, youth, and the Canadian Legion, and for schedules of Masses, Rosary, candlelight processions, community prayer, organ concerts, etc.

The Mary, Queen of Peace pilgrimages leave Quebec City and Montreal to arrive at the Cape for the Feast of the Assumption (August 15). For information write to Mary, Queen of Peace Pilgrimage, 12091, Lacordaire, #2, Montreal North, QC H1G 4L3. After July 1, write to 2590 Pie IX Boulevard, #4, Montreal, QC H1V 2E7.

For your convenience: The grounds are fully equipped and include a cafeteria, infirmary, bookstore and gift shop. For accommodations by the grounds, write to Reservations, Pilgrimage Office, 620 Notre-Dame Street, Cap-de-la-Madeleine, QC G8T 4G9. ☎ and ▤ (819) 374-2441; Lodgings can also be found in the surrounding town of Cap-de-la-Madeleine and in Trois-Rivières.

For further information: Pilgrimage Office, Our Lady of the Cape Shrine, 626 Notre-Dame Street, Cap-de-la-Madeleine, QC G8T 4G9. ☎ and 🖳 (819) 374-2441; e-mail: <u>pelerinages@sanctuaire-ndc.ca</u>; web site: <u>www.sanctuaire-ndc.ca</u>. Regular news of the shrine appears in the periodical *Notre-Dame-du-Cap*, which is published in French. For a subscription write to Notre-Dame-du-Cap, 626 Notre-Dame Street, Cap-de-la-Madeleine, QC G8T 4G9. ☎ and 🖳 (819) 374-2441.

Also of interest: The tomb of Blessed Frédéric Janssoone is in the Chapel of St. Anthony in Trois-Rivières. (See separate entry.) The Cathedral of Trois-Rivières has windows by Guido Nincheri, while the Church of St. Philip has paintings by Légaré and Frère Luc. The beautiful Ursuline Convent houses a large museum and a chapel worthy of a visit.

CARLETON

Oratory of Notre-Dame-du-Mont-Saint-Joseph

Carleton is on the south shore of the Gaspé Peninsula on the Bay of Chaleur. Take Highway 132. The shrine is on a plateau on top of Mont Saint-Joseph, the highest mountain of the region, and can be reached by a serpentine road.

History

From early times the Acadian settlers had erected crosses on the mountain. But in 1925 some parishioners erected a statue of Saint Joseph and the name of the mountain was changed to Mont Saint-Joseph. In 1935 an oratory was built.

In the Marian Year of 1954 the local people responded to Pope Pius XII's wish that Marian shrines be constructed in every type of terrain, even mountain tops. They built a statue of Our Lady of the Assumption, patroness of the Acadians. In 1958 Bishop Bernier of Gaspé blessed and dedicated the shrine to Mary, Queen of the World, and made it a diocesan shrine.

The Shrine

The original fieldstone chapel was built in the style of a Breton pilgrimage chapel, but its style was changed completely by several additions. On the roof is a pedestal with the statue of the Madonna. This, as well as the roof of the church, is outlined in light at night.

The interior is finished in very light-coloured marble. In the apse is a large mosaic triptych of the Queenship of Mary. Among the works of art are some unusual stained glass windows that illustrate Marian shrines around the world, including Washington, La Paz, Tokyo and Ephesus.

To Help You Plan Your Pilgrimage

Schedule: The shrine is open from June 20 to September 15. There are special outdoor Masses for the Feast of the Assumption (August 15) and a week later for the Feast of the Queenship of Mary (August 22). On the Feast of the Assumption there is the Blessing of the Sick. Masses are celebrated on Saturdays and Sundays and may be requested by pilgrim groups.

For your convenience: There are washrooms, an information office, a religious articles counter and parking. Everything is accessible to the handicapped. On the grounds are two telescopes for spectacular views of the coastal region. There are hotels and camping in the village of Carleton. There are restaurants and places for a picnic in Carleton also.

For further information: Saint-Joseph Parish, P.O. Box 268, Carleton, QC G0C 1J0. ☎ (418) 364-3972. In winter, the hours are Tuesday, Thursday and Friday from 1:30 to 4:30 p.m.; in summer, it is open Sundays as well.

Also of interest: The Church of St. Joseph, built in 1860, has a fine tabernacle attributed to François Baillairgé. West along Highway 132 is the Shrine of Ste. Anne de Restigouche. (See separate entry.) A few kilometres northeast of Carleton is the Micmac reservation with a church in the shape of a teepee.

CHERTSEY

Chapel of Mary, Queen of Hearts

Chertsey is 35 kilometres west of Joliette. Take Highway 158 southwest to Saint-Esprit and then Highway 125 northwest.

The Chapel of Mary, Queen of Hearts is run by the Holy Apostles Fathers. On the first Saturday of every month between May and October there are Marian devotions at the chapel.

Also of interest: In nearby Joliette you will find the Provincial House of the Clerics of St. Viateur that houses many works of art, and the cathedral with paintings by Canadian artist Ozias Leduc.

CHICOUTIMI-NORD

Shrine of Ste. Anne
Chicoutimi-Nord is on the north shore of the Saguenay River opposite Chicoutimi. Take the Dubuc Bridge to 2594 Roussel Street. The Shrine of Ste. Anne is in the church of the same name facing the Saguenay River.

The Shrine
The first pilgrimage was in 1878. In 1892 the shrine received a relic of Ste. Anne from Ste. Anne de Beaupré, and the pilgrimage became regional in 1895. Today the beautiful stone church has a statue of Ste. Anne on a tall pedestal in front of it and another statue of her inside.

To Help You Plan Your Pilgrimage

Schedule: From July 16 to 25 there is a novena in preparation for the Feast of Ste. Anne (July 26). On the feast day there are Masses every hour in the morning and three afternoon Masses, including one for the sick. The last of the two evening Masses is followed by a candlelight procession to the cross on top of Cap Saint-Joseph.

For further information: Shrine of Ste. Anne, 2594 Roussel Street, Chicoutimi-North, QC G7G 1Y1. ☎ (418) 543-6091; 🖶 (418) 545-7521.

Also of interest: The cathedral and seminary of Chicoutimi have many paintings by Charles Huot. There are shrines at Lac Bouchette, Alma and Cap Trinité. (See separate entries.) The Chicoutimi area is excellent for modern church architecture: Ste-Cécile at Kénogami, St-Gérard at Larouche, St-Mathias at Arvida and the funnel-like Notre-Dame-de-Fatima at Jonquière.

DESCHAMBAULT

Calvary

Deschambault is on the St. Lawrence River between Trois-Rivières and Quebec City. Take Highway 138, and at Exit 254 turn onto Highway 40. The Calvary, sculpted by Léandre Parent in 1841, is in an outdoor pavilion. The Church of St-Joseph and the rectory are historic.

GUÉRIN

Shrine of St. Gabriel

Guérin is north of Ville-Marie in northwest Quebec, near the Ontario border. From Ville-Marie take Highway 101 north. After Notre-Dame-du-Nord, take the first side road east to Guérin. This little shrine is at the parish church run by the Oblate Order and is the centre for pilgrimage for the region northeast of Lake Temiscamingue.

ILETS-JÉRÉMIE

Ste. Anne's Chapel and Shrine

Ilets-Jérémie is situated on the north shore of the St. Lawrence River, 120 kilometres northeast of Tadoussac. From Quebec City, take Highway 138. There are daily buses from Quebec City and from Sept-Iles.

History

Ilets-Jérémie was the first mission the Jesuits established on the north shore of the St. Lawrence past Tadoussac. They remained there from 1640 to 1782, when the mission was taken over first by diocesan priests and then by Oblates in the 19th century. The mission closed in 1853.

In 1939 Father Arthur Gallant, parish priest of Ste-Thérèse at Colombier, had a reconstruction made of the 18th-century chapel that once stood at Ilets-Jérémie. He called it the Ste. Anne Chapel; it still stands on the top of the cliff. Inside it is the original altar from the chapel of 1735 and many old church furnishings. Next to the church is a tiny but old cemetery. On the grounds is an indoor-outdoor sanctuary.

To Help You Plan Your Pilgrimage

Schedule: The sanctuary and old chapel are open to pilgrims every day during the novena to Ste. Anne (July 15-25) and on the Feast of Ste. Anne (July 26).

For your convenience: The nearest hotel accommodations are at Forestville and Baie-Comeau. There is camping on the shrine grounds.

For further information: Ste-Thérèse-de-Colombier Parish, P.O. Box 139, Colombier, QC G0H 1P0.

Also of interest: Tadoussac, to the southwest at the mouth of the Saguenay River, was the site of the first Christian mission in Canada around 1600. The present chapel was built in 1747.

KAHNAWAKE

Shrine of Kateri Tekakwitha

The Shrine of Kateri is part of the historic Jesuit Mission of St. Francis Xavier on the Indian Reservation at Kahnawake on the St. Lawrence River, facing the southwestern side of Montreal Island. From downtown Montreal, take Sherbrooke Street to Highway 138 and turn right at the shrine sign once you have crossed the Mercier Bridge.

The Lily of the Mohawk

Kateri was born in 1656 at Ossernenon (present-day Auriesville, New York) of a Christian Algonquin mother and a Mohawk father. At four she lost her parents to smallpox. Later when her uncle, a great chief, and other relatives sought a husband for her, she refused and asked to be baptized by Jesuit Father de Lamberville in 1675.

In 1677 Kateri fled from her Mohawk relatives to St. Francis Xavier Mission on the St. Lawrence River. There she became well known for her spirituality. She died in 1680 at the age of 24 and miracles began almost at once.

In 1980, on the 300th anniversary of her death, she was declared "Blessed" by Pope John Paul II. Today the Kateri Movement is encouraging the integration of native traditional spirituality within the liturgy.

History

In 1667 the Jesuits established the Mission of St. Francis Xavier at La Prairie and eventually moved it to Kahnawake in 1717. In 1725 the French built Fort St. Louis to protect the mission from attack.

The old church was demolished in 1845 and the present one built. The shrine of Kateri was set up in a transept of the church in 1972 when her remains were moved here.

The Shrine and Mission

The parish church of Kahnawake is of local stone with a silver bell-tower and steeple in the traditional Quebec style. The high altar and two matching side altars are elaborately carved in a classical style with fluted Corinthian columns supporting entablatures.

The large wooden crucifix below the baldachino was donated by 35 Kahnawake widows to commemorate their husbands who were killed in the collapse of the Quebec Bridge in 1907. The statue of Kateri Tekakwitha over the tabernacle was carved by Leo Arbour.

The scenes of the life of Christ on the barrel vaults were painted by Florentine artist Guido Nincheri. Note the large paintings given to the mission by King Charles X of France around 1825. Note also the Stations of the Cross with their Iroquois captions.

The tomb of Blessed Kateri is in the right transept of the church. It is made of white Carrara marble. On it are the incised name and outlines of a lily and a turtle. Just behind the tomb is a statue of Kateri by Médard Bourgault. Nearby is a painting of Kateri and the children of the world by Arizona artist Marlene McCauley, whose own child was cured through the intercession of Kateri.

The sacristy with its reredos, the little museum and the two 18th-century stone mission buildings are worth a visit. Beyond the mission compound are the remnants of the fort.

To Help You Plan Your Pilgrimage

Schedule: The shrine is open all year. There are Masses each day and on Sunday mornings. Pilgrim groups of 20 or more may request a local priest in advance. Groups having their own priest may request a Mass time in advance.

For your convenience: The parking lot is across from the church. There are washrooms on the premises and a shop of religious articles and Native handicrafts. Accommodations can be found in Montreal. There is one tiny restaurant and a pizza parlour on the reserve.

For further information: Shrine of Kateri, P.O. Box 70, Kahnawake, QC J0L 1B0. ☎ (450) 632-6030; 🖳 (450) 632-6031. For current news on shrine activities, a quarterly magazine, *Kateri*, is published.

Also of interest: There is a small museum on the reservation. The McCord Museum on Sherbrooke Street in Montreal offers a look at Native Canadian History as well.

LA FERME

Shrine of Notre-Dame-de-l'Assomption

La Ferme or St. Viateur de la Ferme is in northwestern Quebec (Abitibi), toward the Ontario border. It is on Lac Beauchamp near Amos. From Amos take Highway 395 west about 10 kilometres.

This part of Quebec was late being settled. In 1917 the Federal Government set up an experimental farm here, the source of the name La Ferme. In 1936 the Clerics of Saint Viateur set up an agricultural school and, two years later, the Parish of St. Viateur.

The Shrine of Notre-Dame-de-l'Assomption began in 1940 when three religious brothers placed tiny statues of Our Lady of Lourdes and St. Joseph on a rock behind the parish church.

The first pilgrimage took place in 1942. In 1955 a beautiful granite chapel with one side open was established. Inside it is a statue of Our Lady of the Assumption.

To Help You Plan Your Pilgrimage

Schedule: There is an annual diocesan pilgrimage on the Sunday closest to the Feast of the Assumption (August 15). The shrine is open in spring, summer and fall from 9:00 a.m. to 9:00 p.m.

For further information: Our Lady of the Assumption Shrine, R.R. #4, P.O. Box 4196, Amos, La Ferme, QC J9T 3A3. ☎ (819) 732-4637; ▤ (819) 732-7048.

Also of interest: Within 160 kilometres of Ville-Marie are shrines at Guérin, Roquemaure, the Cathedral of St. Michael at Rouyn-Noranda, and the beautiful Gothic Church of St. Martin in the mining town of Malartic. The Byzantine-style Cathedral of St. Teresa of Avila at Amos is worth a visit.

LA POCATIÈRE

Shrine of Our Lady of Fatima

La Pocatière is east of Quebec City on the south shore of the St. Lawrence River. The shrine is on Highway 132 between Exits 436 and 439 of the Trans-Canada Highway, northwest of La Pocatière.

Fatima

In 1917, near the village of Fatima, Portugal, three shepherd children saw an apparition of a woman. She asked them to say the Rosary daily for the conversion of sinners and for peace in the world (World War I was in progress). Each time the children returned the crowds grew. At the sixth and last apparition, 70,000 people were present and a great prodigy occurred – the sun was seen to dance through the sky. A shrine to Our Lady of Fatima was constructed and became world famous.

History

In 1946, while the statue of Our Lady of Fatima was on a world tour, someone placed a statuette of the Virgin on a spot of land where the students of the Collège de Ste-Anne-de-la-Pocatière used to gather in warm weather. Many people began coming here to pray. In 1950 statues of Our Lady of Fatima and the three children carved by Médard Bourgault and others were installed and blessed. In 1952 a kiosk with an altar for celebration of Mass was set up. The shrine is outdoors with rows of pews in a well-landscaped area.

To Help You Plan Your Pilgrimage

Schedule: The pilgrimage season is July and August. There is a pilgrimage for the elderly on the Feast of the Queenship of Mary (August 22). Masses at the shrine are on Sunday mornings (July and August) and Wednesday afternoons (June to September), when the Rosary is included. The Rosary is prayed on Sunday afternoons (June to September). An organized group may reserve in advance.

For your convenience: There are accommodations and restaurants in La Pocatière.

For further information: Our Lady of Fatima Shrine, Shrine Director, P.O. Box 430, La Pocatière, QC G0R 1Z0. ☎ (418) 856-1811; 🖳 (418) 856-5863; e-mail: <u>diocesap@globetrotter.qc.ca</u>.

Also of interest: The modern Cathedral of La Pocatière is interesting. The parish church of St-Jean-Port-Joli is worth a visit. (See separate entry.)

The Novalis Guide to Canadian Shrines

LAC-AU-SAUMON

Chapelle Saint-Joseph

Lac-au-Saumon is an Acadian community on the Matapedia River, southeast of Mont-Joli in the Gaspé.

The little shrine was founded in 1921. It is open for private devotions every day from May to September. During this season there is a Mass every Wednesday.

LAC-BOUCHETTE

Hermitage of St. Anthony of Padua

From Quebec City take Highway 175 north, then Highway 169. At Chambord take Highway 155 north for the final 20 kilometres. From Montreal take Highway 55 and Highway 155 north.

The Hermitage is one of the largest shrines in Canada and the only large one devoted to St. Anthony of Padua. Of equal importance here is devotion to Our Lady of Lourdes.

St. Anthony of Padua

St. Anthony of Padua (1195–1231) was born in Lisbon, Portugal, of a noble family. Unhappy with the religious spirit of his monastery where he had become an expert in Scripture, he joined the Franciscans in Morocco in 1220 and eventually ended up in Italy. A famous preacher, he preached to huge crowds in Italy and France and died at Padua at age 36. Anthony is venerated as the apostle of charity to the poor and as patron of lovers, marriage, pregnant women and miners. He is especially popular as the finder of lost objects. St. Anthony's Bread is a fund for assistance to the poor.

History

The founder of the Hermitage of St. Anthony of Padua at Lac-Bouchette, Father Elzéar Delamarre, developed a special interest in St. Anthony on a visit to Italy. Upon his return to Canada he bought a hillside site on the north shore of Lac-Bouchette as a summer place of retreat for seminary professors, and he built a chalet and a tiny chapel dedicated to St. Anthony.

66

In 1915 the first organized group of pilgrims arrived. In 1917, while improvements were being made to the property, a natural grotto resembling the Lourdes grotto was found, and a shrine to Our Lady of Lourdes was established. Hardly was it blessed when the first cures were reported.

In 1925 Father Delamarre died and the Capuchin Fathers took charge. In 1948 they built their monastery on the grounds and in 1950 a new Lourdes Chapel.

The Shrine

The shrine grounds are along the shore of the lake, a place of great tranquility. The old Chapel of St. Anthony is made of wood in the Gothic style and has a bell-tower and a delicate-looking spire. Inside, above the Gothic altar, is the statue of St. Anthony carrying the child Jesus. On the walls, flanking the altar, are some *ex-votos*.

Above the altar is a painting of St. Anthony – "cause of charity to the poor, cause of the defeat of the serpent of evil." This and 22 other paintings on the life of St. Anthony are by Charles Huot (1855–1930), a Canadian artist who studied with Cabanel in Paris. In front of the altar is a stone plaque marking the grave of Father Delamarre.

At the entrance to the extensive grounds is the carved and painted wooden Calvary group by Louis Jobin. Along a path through the woods is a beautiful stone Way of the Cross carved by R. Goffin of Chicoutimi. The north side of the grounds is dominated by the Monastery of the Capuchins, with a massive lookout tower in the Romanesque style. Further up the hill on the highest part of the property is the modern Marian Chapel.

The chapel was designed by architect Henri Tremblay in the shape of a semi-cylindrical shell. At the side entrance is the stone bell-tower, unusual in that it doesn't rise above the roof line of the church. The facade of the church is mainly glass but in the centre of the facade is a niche with a gigantic stone statue of the Virgin Mary. Inside the church are stained glass windows in abstract designs. There are shrines here to both St. Anthony and Our Lady.

From the terrace in front of the church a long stone stair-case descends the hillside to the level of the lake. The space here can accommodate large crowds for open-air liturgies. To the left of the altar is a grey stone building with a classical facade. Inside is a replica of the shrine of the *Scala Sancta* in Rome. Farther left is the natural Grotto of Our Lady of Lourdes with a spring nearby.

To Help You Plan Your Pilgrimage

Schedule: The shrine is open from Holy Week to the end of October. The Feast of St. Anthony is June 13. Over 300 organized groups come here on pilgrimage every year. Please write for schedules of Masses, novenas, candlelight processions, the blessing of the lilies, the blessing of St. Anthony's Bread, and the Third Orders pilgrimage.

For your convenience: The shrine is fully equipped. From late June to early August there is often theatre in the evening. For accommodations on the grounds, write to Hotel de la Grotte Ltée, 250, route de l'Ermitage, Lac-Bouchette, QC G0W 1V0. ☎ (418) 348-6344 or 1-800-868-6344; 🖳 (418) 348-9463; e-mail: ermitage@st-antoine.org; web site: www.st-antoine.org.

For further information: Hermitage of Saint Anthony, 250, route de l'Ermitage, Lac-Bouchette, QC G0W 1V0. ☎ (418) 348-6344. *Le Messager de Saint-Antoine*, the shrine's French-language monthly magazine, gives current news of the shrine and its work.

Also of interest: There are shrines at Alma, Chicoutimi-North and Cap Trinité. (See separate entries.) Roberval has a Brébeuf Park with sculptures of the Canadian Martyrs. At Mistassini is a Cistercian abbey where the monks have invented chocolate-covered blueberries for the local August blueberry festival. The museums at Mistassini and Péribonka are worth seeing.

LAC-ETCHEMIN

Shrine of Notre-Dame d'Etchemin

Lac Etchemin is on the south side of the St. Lawrence River, southeast of Quebec City. From Lévis take Highways 173 and 277 south. The shrine is on the southwest shore of the lake.

The Shrine

This shrine was founded in 1952 by Father Adrien Ouellet to encourage local popular devotions. The church is built of wood in a rustic style. There is a spire and the windows and entrance are Gothic. There are four tiny rose windows. The location is beautiful – between two groves of trees on the south side of the lake facing the Church of Ste-Germaine across the lake. There are gardens here with a Way of the Cross. Inside the church is the statue of Notre-Dame d'Etchemin designed by artist Guido Casini.

To Help You Plan Your Pilgrimage

Schedule: The Feast of the Birth of Mary (September 8) is still the main pilgrimage day and pilgrims come from all over the province and beyond. The feast is preceded by a novena. The Feast of the Assumption (August 15) is also a pilgrimage day.

For further information: L'Oeuvre du Sanctuaire Notre-Dame d'Etchemin, 195 2nd Avenue, Lac-Etchemin QC G0R 1S0.

LACHUTE

Grotto of Our Lady of Lourdes

Lachute is not far from the Ottawa River in County Argenteuil. It is just west of Montreal on Highway 148. The shrine is on Highway 327 outside Lachute on the way to Brownsburg.

History

In 1929 Madame Bernadette Ayers went to Lourdes, France, with her three daughters, the eldest of whom, Eva Pearl, had heart problems. On returning to Canada, mother and daughters thought to recreate the atmosphere of Lourdes on a hillside property they owned near Lachute. Madame Ayers was encouraged by her uncle, pastor at Masson, who gave her a relic of St. Bernadette. When Eva Pearl became very ill she persuaded her mother to set up statues of Mary and Bernadette on the land, but she died before the statues were blessed. The next year,

1936, Madame Ayers had the hillside landscaped and in 1949 she gave the shrine to the Franciscans.

The Shrine

The shrine is organized like a formal garden up the side of the hill. At the entrance is an arched gateway in wrought iron. At the end of the path is a statue of Jesus of the Sacred Heart. The path to the left leads to the church, while to the right is the Lourdes chapel and the Franciscan Monastery behind it.

Continuing up the hill the path divides again. To the left and right are paths through the woods. Straight ahead are two staircases that bring you to the terrace of the Grotto of Our Lady of Lourdes. There are benches here and a delightful view of the surrounding hills.

To Help You Plan Your Pilgrimage

Schedule: The Lourdes chapel with its tiny belfry is open day and night for private prayer. Masses are celebrated in the large modern church.

Please note that there are no special pilgrimage days and that the shrine does not help to organize pilgrimages. The shrine grounds are open all year. Anyone who wishes to consult a priest may do so at any time at the monastery.

For your convenience: There is a place for picnicking on the shrine grounds.

Also of interest: At least three villages in the Laurentian resort area north of here have placed an illuminated cross on a nearby mountaintop: Ste-Adèle, Ste-Agathe-des-Monts and St-Donat.

LORETTEVILLE

Huron Chapel of Notre-Dame-de-Lorette

The chapel is on the Wendake Huron Reserve at Loretteville, north of Sillery and on the edge of metropolitan Quebec City.

Though no longer used as a shrine, it is worth a visit because it is among the oldest Canadian shrines (along with Quebec's Our Lady of the Victories and the chapel at Cap-de-la-Madeleine).

The first chapel was built in 1673 at nearby Ancienne-Lorette for the Hurons who had fled the Iroquois attacks on Huronia. It was named by Jesuit Father Pierre Chaumonot, who had been cured at the Shrine of the Holy House of Loreto, Italy. The second chapel, the present one at Loretteville, was built in 1730 after the Indians had moved here. Many of the colonists of New France as well as the Hurons used to come here on pilgrimage.

Also of interest: There is a small museum here.

LOURDES-DE-BLANC-SABLON

Shrine of Notre-Dame-de-Lourdes

Blanc-Sablon is on the north shore of the Gulf of St. Lawrence near the Labrador border. There are no roads connecting the community with the rest of Quebec but there is a road (Highway 510) on the Labrador side. There is also a ferry from Saint-Barbe, Newfoundland. For the more adventurous there is a three-day coastal boat from Sept-Iles that stops at such out-of-the-way places as Anticosti Island. Lourdes is northwest of Blanc-Sablon.

In 1917 a wooden statue of Our Lady of Lourdes, made in France, was placed in a newly constructed kiosk on top of the rugged hill known as Cape Crow. It was blessed by Eudist Father François Hesry. Most of the additions to the shrine were made during the Marian Year of 1987–88.

On top of the pavilion is a cross that is lighted at night. On the hillside are the letters AVE almost three metres high and also lighted at night. On the right, at the foot of the hill, is a Stations of the Cross that was made in Italy. On the left side of the hill is the fishermen's giant Rosary designed by an Oblate artist, Father Toby McGivern, with a boat in the centre of it.

To Help You Plan Your Pilgrimage

Schedule: The devotion of the living Rosary is very popular here, particularly in the months of May and October.

Also of interest: At the Church of Notre-Dame-de-Lourdes is a little museum in honour of Oblate Bishop Scheffer, first bishop of Labrador City and Schefferville.

MAYO

Shrine of Our Lady of Knock

The Shrine of Our Lady of Knock is in the beautiful hilly woodland of West Quebec. Mayo is only 45 kilometres from Ottawa-Hull. From Hull take Highway 50 east to Masson, then the last exit to Highway 309 north to Buckingham. Take Highway 315 north to Mayo.

History

Mayo, Quebec, is named for the Irish county in which the village of Knock (Cnoc) is situated. Many of the original settlers in this part of Quebec came from County Mayo. In the early 1950s Mayo's parish priest, Father Clement Braceland, went to Ireland to visit the shrine of Knock where, in 1879, 15 villagers witnessed a silent apparition of the Virgin on the church gable. He came home determined to build a replica. The new shrine was designed by Ottawa artist Bruno Duchesi and blessed in 1955 by Archbishop Lemieux of Ottawa.

The Shrine

The shrine is attached to the side of the church of St. Malachy. Celebrations are held outdoors. There is an open-work kiosk to Mary on the grounds.

To Help You Plan Your Pilgrimage

Schedule: Pilgrimage season is the warmer months. The Feast of the Assumption (August 15 if a Sunday, or the Sunday before August 15) is the annual pilgrimage day. In the morning there is Reconciliation and Mass followed by lunch. In the afternoon there is Rosary, a procession to the cemetery followed by the Blessing of the Sick and religious articles, and finally a Mass for the sick. Pilgrimage groups may make private arrangements for other days.

For your convenience: There is some outdoor seating, but bring a folding chair. There is a bed-and-breakfast site less than 2 kilometres from Mayo, and motels between Mayo and Buckingham.

For further information: Our Lady of Victory Parish, 490 Charles Street, Buckingham, QC J8L 2K5. ☎ (819) 986-3763; 🖳 (819) 986-9889.

Also of interest: Not far to the northwest is the Shrine of Notre-Dame-de-la-Salette. (See separate entry.)

MONT-JOLI

Grotto of Notre-Dame-de-Lourdes

Mont-Joli is on the south shore of the St. Lawrence River, northeast of Rimouski at the western limit of the Highway 132 that circles the Gaspé Peninsula.

The grotto, beautifully constructed of local stone in 1928, is situated on a hillside right in front of the Church of Notre-Dame-de-Lourdes. There is a spring here and an altar in the cave for outdoor Mass. Mass is celebrated daily in the parish church.

Lodgings can be found in Mont-Joli.

To the southwest at Pointe-au-Père is the Shrine of Ste. Anne. (See separate entry.)

MONTREAL

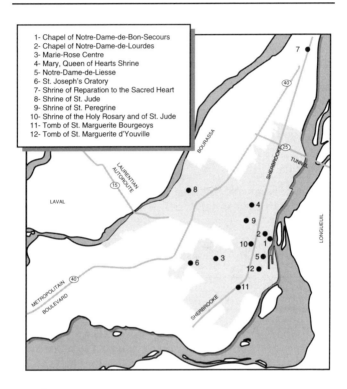

1- Chapel of Notre-Dame-de-Bon-Secours
2- Chapel of Notre-Dame-de-Lourdes
3- Marie-Rose Centre
4- Mary, Queen of Hearts Shrine
5- Notre-Dame-de-Liesse
6- St. Joseph's Oratory
7- Shrine of Reparation to the Sacred Heart
8- Shrine of St. Jude
9- Shrine of St. Peregrine
10- Shrine of the Holy Rosary and of St. Jude
11- Tomb of St. Marguerite Bourgeoys
12- Tomb of St. Marguerite d'Youville

Marie-Rose Centre

The Marie-Rose Centre is in Outremont near Mount Royal.

Blessed Marie-Rose

Born Eulalie Durocher at St. Antoine on the Richelieu River in 1811, Mother Marie-Rose was the tenth child of prosperous farmers. Together with Bishop Bourget of Montreal, she saw the great need for teachers for poor rural children. With Bishop Bourget's support she founded a Canadian community, the Sisters of the Holy Names of Jesus and Mary.

Despite initial disapproval from her own family, she moved to Longueuil and founded the order in 1843. Mother Marie-Rose and her sisters lived in poverty and taught poor children.

She proved to be an excellent model of religious life and a good administrator. But the poor health she had for much of her life began to take its toll and she died in 1849 at the age of 38. She was beatified in 1982. Today her community continues to teach and do pastoral work in Canada and in five other countries.

The Shrine

Today the Marie-Rose Centre is in the Motherhouse of her order. The tomb of Marie-Rose was moved here in 1925 from the cemetery of the old Motherhouse in Longueuil.

To Help You Plan Your Pilgrimage

Schedule: The centre is open all year. In winter, the hours are Tuesday to Friday from 9:00 to 11:30 a.m. and from 1:00 to 3:00 p.m.; in summer, it is open Sundays as well. Visitors should make arrangements in advance. The magnificent chapel was modelled on the Basilica of St. Mary Major in Rome. There is a little museum on the life and work of Marie-Rose. Group visits include a video on the life of Marie-Rose, a visit to the museum and a visit to the tomb.

For further information: Director, Marie-Rose Centre, 1420 Mont-Royal Boulevard, Montreal, QC H2V 2J2. ☎ (450) 651-8104; 🖷 (450) 651-8636; e-mail: snjmga@=.net; web site: www.snjm.qc.ca.

Also of interest: Nearby is Mount Royal's illuminated cross, the largest of its kind in the world, and St. Joseph's Oratory. (See separate entry.)

Chapel of Notre-Dame-de-Bon-Secours (Our Lady of Good Help)

The chapel is at 400 Saint-Paul Street East, in the old part of Montreal. The oldest church in Montreal, it is next to the old domed market building.

History

Marguerite Bourgeoys (1620–1700), one of the most energetic people in early Montreal, had the first stone for the church blessed in 1657. When interest languished, Marguerite obtained a small carved statue of Notre-Dame-de-Bon-Secours in 1672 and placed it in an outdoor wooden oratory. The first chapel was finally finished in 1678 and the statue was moved inside.

In 1754 the chapel burned but the statue was found intact in the ruins. In 1773 the chapel was rebuilt and the statue reinstalled in a place of honour. Between 1885 and 1910 both the exterior and the interior of the chapel were restored and the tower with the huge copper statue of Mary overlooking the harbour was built.

The Chapel

The grey stone facade of the church is in the neo-classical style. The interior is elaborately decorated with many stained glass windows, mosaics, paintings and sculptures. The high altar and two side altars are a match, with intricately-carved marble scenes from the life of Christ and Mary.

On the left side of the church is enshrined the tiny statue of Notre-Dame de Bon-Secours that Marguerite brought from France in 1672. Here is a recumbent figure of Marguerite and a relic. Before leaving the church, have a look at the model ships suspended from the ceiling and carrying vigil lights. These are *ex-votos* given by sailors in thanksgiving for safe voyages.

On the main level is a religious articles shop and, in the basement, a tiny museum. Go up the winding staircase to the two galleries in the tower to have a great view of the harbour and the rooftops of Old Montreal.

To Help You Plan Your Pilgrimage

Schedule: The church is open year round. Mass is celebrated every day, and every Saturday morning there is a pilgrimage Mass to Mary preceded by the Rosary. Throughout May there is an evening Marian devotion on weekdays. The Feast of the Assumption is celebrated on the Sunday immediately following August 15. Beginning in the early afternoon there is a procession with the miraculous statue followed by the Rosary and Mass.

Also of interest: Don't miss the magnificent Basilica of Notre-Dame on Place d'Armes and next to it the Sulpician seminary, the oldest building in Montreal. At 138 St. Pierre Street is the former Youville Motherhouse where St. Marguerite d'Youville and her Grey Nuns first lived. The tomb of St. Marguerite Bourgeoys is in Westmount. (See separate entry.)

Chapel of Notre-Dame-de-Lourdes

A good example of an urban shrine, the chapel is on busy St. Catherine Street (between St-Denis and Berri Streets). Surrounded by the University of Quebec, it is close to the bus and subway stations. There are no shrine grounds, just a church. But this church is a jewel in a city of beautiful churches.

History

In the 1860s there were so many religious confraternities using the old Gothic Cathedral of Saint-Jacques that it became clear that they needed their own chapel. A rich member of one of these confraternities, Côme Cherrier, agreed to donate land across the street from Saint-Jacques, providing the chapel would be dedicated to the Virgin of the Immaculate Conception. A fundraising drive was begun and Napoléon Bourassa was named architect and decorator.

The Shrine

From St. Catherine Street the most noticeable thing about the church is the gold-leaf-covered statue of the Virgin Mary on the gable. The building is in a Romanesque-Byzantine style and is unusual in being an architectural and decorative ensemble – one artist was allowed to develop his ideas with consistency.

The facade, in alternating grey and white stone, has a rose window and many double Romanesque windows. There is a Byzantine-style dome with a lantern over the crossing and semi-domes at the ends of the transept and in the apse. The church is lighted by arched windows high up by the barrel vault and at the base of the dome. There are no lower-storey windows. There are side aisles, a short nave and short transepts.

The eye is directed immediately to the sanctuary and to the high altar. Over the domed tabernacle is a carved and gilded Romanesque triumphal arch. In the archway, lighted by hidden windows, is a statue of Our Lady of Lourdes carved by Louis-Philippe Hébert. At the base of the altar are two bas-reliefs by Hébert – the Incarnation and Mary giving Jesus to the world. Flanking the altar are two large standing gilt-bronze candelabra with winged dragons on their bases.

On the ceiling of the sanctuary are paintings of saints of the New Testament who spoke of the Immaculate Conception. These are matched in the vault of the nave by the four Old Testament women who prefigured Mary. In the centre of the vault of the nave are the four grisaille paintings of Mary in Glory. In the centre of the dome is Mary enthroned.

The lower walls of the transepts and aisles are painted in the *trompe-l'œil* fashion to look like arched windows open to the blue sky. In the transepts are statues of St. Michael and St. John the Evangelist by Hébert. Around the walls of the aisles are tiny plaques of the Stations of the Cross by Elzéar Soucy.

To Help You Plan Your Pilgrimage

Schedule: The shrine is open all year, at all times. The Feast of the Assumption (August 15) and the Feast of the Immaculate Conception (December 8) are both celebrated with special Masses.

There are Masses and Rosary daily and the shrine is open every afternoon for Adoration of the Blessed Sacrament.

For further information: Notre-Dame-de-Lourdes Chapel, 430 St. Catherine Street East, Montreal, QC H2L 2C5. ☎ phone (514) 845-8278; 🖳 (514) 845-8279.

Also of interest: The Shrine of the Rosary and St. Jude is on St. Denis Street. (See separate entry.) Along Henri-Julien Avenue are three churches with magnificently decorated interiors: St-Jean Baptiste (at 4237, corner of Rachel Street), Notre-Dame-de-la-Défense (at 6800, corner of Dante, south of Bélanger Street), and St-Vincent Ferrier (at 8115, corner of Jarry Street). These Montreal church interiors are Canada's best-kept secret.

Mary, Queen of Hearts Shrine

Mary, Queen of Hearts

St. Louis de Montfort (1673–1716), founder of the Missionary Company of Mary (Montfort Fathers and Brothers), lived in a poverty-stricken ghetto in the City of Poitiers. Because of their poverty the people of the ghetto did not feel at home in the parish church. In the middle of the quarter was a large shed used for meetings and dances. Louis convinced the people to use it as a prayer hall and preached a retreat in it. At the end of the retreat Louis asked them to offer their hearts to Jesus through Mary. Many laid wooden and metal ex-voto hearts around the statue of Mary and committed themselves to return to contem-

plate their hearts and pray to Mary. Montfort decided to leave the statue there as a memorial to the retreat and it soon became known as Mary, Queen of Hearts.

The shrine is at 5875 Sherbrooke Street East at Bossuet Street.

The Shrine

The shrine, founded by the Montfort Fathers in 1958 and finished in 1960, is in a 1950s modern style. The roof is like a piece of pleated paper and from it hangs an upper wall of stained glass windows, almost like curtains. The tall, beautifully designed bell-tower incorporates a blue cross on all four of its sides.

Near the main entrance is a huge statue of St. Louis de Montfort, the pilgrim with a pack on his back. It was cast in bronze by Dutch sculptor Josef Zanzmaier in 1966. Inside the shrine there is seating for 1,200 people.

On the gold mosaic altar on the right side of the church is the Shrine of Mary, Queen of Hearts. Built of white marble, it shows the kneeling St. Louis de Montfort presenting a heart to the enthroned Madonna and Child.

At the entrance to the church is a circular votary chapel with a blue ceramic pillar containing another version of the statue of Mary, Queen of Hearts. Circling the pillar are many levels of vigil lights. Downstairs is the crypt church where every Sunday a special Mass is celebrated with a small orchestra. Also here is a six-sided memorial chapel.

To Help You Plan Your Pilgrimage

Schedule: The shrine is open from 6:00 a.m. to 8:00 p.m. Monday to Saturday, and Sunday 7:30 a.m. to 6:00 p.m. There are Masses and the Rosary is prayed daily. May is the month of preparation for consecration to Jesus through Mary according to the spirituality of St. Louis de Montfort. In this spirituality March 25 is the day of devotion to the Annunciation. In August there is a preparatory triduum and celebration of the Feast of the Assumption (August 15). The Feast of Our Lady of the Rosary is October 7. There is also a triduum and celebration of the Feast of the Immaculate Conception (December 8).

For your convenience: The shrine is fully equipped, except for food and lodging.

For further information: Shrine of Mary, Queen of Hearts, 4000 Bossuet Street, Montreal, QC H1M 2M2. ☎ (514) 254-5376; 🖷 (514) 254-5378; e-mail: <u>smrdc@qc.aira.com</u>; web site: <u>http:/</u> <u>/smrdc.multimania.com</u>.

Also of interest: To the east in Pointe-aux-Trembles is the Shrine of Reparation to the Sacred Heart. (See separate entry.)

Notre-Dame-de-Liesse

The Shrine of Notre-Dame-de-Liesse is located in the downtown Jesuit Church of the Gesu at 1202 Bleury Street.

History

The Shrine of Notre-Dame-de-Liesse near Laon, France, began in the 12th century and soon became something of a national shrine with many of the kings and queens of France going there on pilgrimage. During the French Revolution the shrine was damaged and the statue of Notre-Dame itself was burned. The ashes, however, were saved. When the shrine re-opened in the early 19th century, a new statue was made and the ashes were placed in a container at the base of this statue. Later, a second statue was made and, in 1877, the older statue was given to two Canadian Jesuits studying in France so that it would be brought to Canada. Since then it has been at the Gesu Church in Montreal.

In the late 19th and early 20th centuries there were many pilgrimages organized and many extraordinary favours reported. Today, though many individual pilgrims still come to the shrine, there are no longer any organized pilgrimages. In 1977 the centenary of the shrine was celebrated with the crowning of the child Jesus on the Madonna's lap.

The Shrine

The Shrine of Notre-Dame-de-Liesse is in the left transept of the church. The statue, seemingly held up by two angels, is enthroned on an elaborately carved stand above the tabernacle of the altar. Above the statue on the wall is a huge mural in grisaille of the Trinity holding a crown for the Virgin Mary. Framing this picture are many silver votive hearts. There are many *ex-voto* marble plaques on the walls of the transept.

The stone Church of the Gesu, built in 1865, has one of the most elaborately decorated interiors in Montreal with many chapels and oratories.

There are several unusual statues made of papier maché and beautifully painted, including one of St. Ignatius of Loyola. Around the inlaid altars are many delightful floor candelabras and hanging sanctuary lamps. The church has a double choirloft and a fine pipe organ with almost 5,000 pipes.

To Help You Plan Your Pilgrimage

Schedule: The church is open all year. The special pilgrimage day is on September 22. There is an evening devotion with Rosary, Mass and special homily on the first Saturday of every month.

For your convenience: There is parking behind the church and washrooms and souvenir stands in the church. For spiritual consultation, inquire at the office.

For further information: Director, Shrine of Notre-Dame-de-Liesse, Church of the Gesu, 1202 Bleury Street, Montreal, QC H3B 3J3.

Also of interest: Not far away on René-Levesque Boulevard is the large Gothic St. Patrick's Basilica and the domed Cathedral of Mary Queen of the World.

Shrine of Reparation to the Sacred Heart

This shrine, near the eastern tip of the island of Montreal, is a real gem. Known locally as La Réparation, it is not well known in English-speaking Canada. Nevertheless, complete information is available in English and many anglophone Canadians and Americans are among the 200,000 people who visit every year.

History

This shrine has the distinction of being founded by a lay woman. Marie de la Rousselière was born at Angers, France, in 1840. This energetic woman grew up in a France marked by strife between monarchists and republicans and the building of the Basilica of the Sacred Heart on Montmartre in Paris in reparation for the sins of the nation. After having been briefly arrested by an anti-clerical government, Marie came to Canada with relatives in 1885 to avoid religious persecution. In 1896, at the suggestion of her nephew (later Father Clément Brisset de Nos), she founded the shrine on some undeveloped land owned by her sister and brother-in-law.

In 1897 a little wooden chapel was dedicated and the outdoor Way of the Cross was built by Father Frédéric Janssoone. In 1901 Marie returned to France and died 23 years later in a Carmelite convent. Others took over her work and completed a stone chapel in 1910.

In 1921 the Capuchins took charge and began building a monastery attached to the church. By the 1950s a larger church had to be built nearby to handle the crowds. In 1984 the Padre Pio Hall was built inside this church for the use of pilgrim groups.

The Shrine

As you enter the grounds the first thing you see is the golden statue of Jesus of the Sacred Heart standing on top of the bell-tower of the old chapel with his arms outstretched in welcome. Over the central doorway of the chapel is a tympanum with the Vision of St. Margaret Mary carved by sculptor Armand Filion.

The inside of the church has been restored. The Shrine of Jesus of the Sacred Heart is over the altar. In the left transept is a sculpted wooden panel showing one of St. Margaret Mary's visions. The daily liturgy and devotions are held in this church.

To the right of the chapel is the Capuchin monastery and to the left is the modern church. The austere auditorium-like interior holds 2,000 people. On the right side of the sanctuary is a Shrine of the Sacred Heart of Jesus.

The Grounds

The first monument one sees on entering the grove is the stained glass, epoxy and metal sculpture to St. Francis, patron of ecology. The most prominent feature along the path is the Way of the Cross by Carli. The impressive life-size bronze Calvary group was placed on the hillock in 1931. You can enter the tiny building that houses the tomb, said to have been built by Father Frédéric with his own hands.

Also in the woods is a Grotto of Our Lady of Lourdes made in 1891, and an open chapel built in 1946 to celebrate the golden jubilee of the shrine. Above the chapel altar is a very fine stone crucifix carved by Armand Filion. There is a clearing in front of the chapel and Mass can be celebrated here by large groups.

Nearby is a delightful little building that houses a reproduction of Rome's Holy Stairs from Pilate's palace. Built in 1904–1905, this little church has a Byzantine look with its dome, half-domes and niches. At the top of the Holy Stairs under a half-dome one finds a dramatic life-size group of the Last Supper.

To Help You Plan Your Pilgrimage

Schedule: The old chapel is open daily from 7:00 a.m. to 9:00 p.m., while the large chapel is open every Sunday. The grove is open from April 1 to the end of October.

The Feast of the Sacred Heart falls on the Friday following the second Sunday after Pentecost, usually in June. This is preceded by a novena with Masses and candlelight processions. On a Saturday in early May the pilgrimage called the Marian Train begins at this shrine. The pilgrims visit many Montreal churches for devotions, finishing at St. Joseph's Oratory. The Good Friday penitential walk ends at the Shrine of Reparation after visits to five other churches.

For your convenience: The shrine is fully equipped.

For further information: Director, Shrine of Reparation to the Sacred Heart, 3650 de la Rousselière Street, Montreal, QC H1A 2X9. ☎ (514) 642-5391; ▤ (514) 642-5033; e-mail: sacre-coeur@videotron.ca; web site: www.novacom.qc.ca/ssc/bienvenue.html. Please write to obtain the shrine's magazine *Le Sauveur* (French language only).

Also of interest: The Church of Notre-Dame-des-Champs at Repentigny is an unusual lyre-shaped building. Nearby Varennes has two shrines. (See separate entries.)

Shrine of St. Jude

The shrine is at 10120 Auteuil Avenue in the Ahuntsic area, north of Metropolitain Boulevard, just west of the Sauvé subway station.

The Church of St. Jude was founded by Cardinal Léger in 1953 and blessed in 1956. The exterior is distinguished by a tall bell-tower with bells from Orléans, France. A statue of St. Jude is in front of the church.

The interior contains a series of fine stained glass windows by Dutch artist Gerald Mesterom. The oratory of St. Jude is near the entrance of the church with a large window behind it and an elaborate arrangement of vigil lights. The statue of St. Jude and the bas-reliefs of Marguerite Bourgeoys and Brother André were sculpted by Laure Sénécal.

To Help You Plan Your Pilgrimage

Schedule: The church is open daily from 9:00 a.m. to 5:00 p.m. A perpetual novena continues every Thursday evening, with the central novena running from October 19 to 28, the Feast of St. Jude.

For further information: St. Jude Parish and Shrine, 10120 Auteuil Avenue, Montreal, QC H3L 2K1. ☎ (514) 381-1767; 🖃 (514) 381-6012.

Shrine of St. Peregrine

One of the newest shrines in Canada, the Shrine of St. Peregrine was established in 1987 at the Church of St-Eusèbe, 2151 Fullum Street (at Larivière Street) in east-central Montreal.

St. Peregrine

St. Peregrine Laziosi (1260–1345) was an Italian Servite preacher. Advanced cancer of his foot was suddenly healed after he had a vision of the crucified Jesus. Canonized in 1726, he is the patron saint of those suffering from cancer.

The Shrine

The stone Church of St-Eusèbe is very large with big copper roofs. Inside, the cavernous nave has a barrel-vaulted ceiling with a series of medallions painted by Guido Nincheri. The extremely elaborate mouldings on the walls and ceilings culminate in eight caryatid-like angels above the columns at the crossing of the nave and transepts. There is a magnificent ciborium over the high altar, a double choir loft and several other galleries.

The altar of St. Peregrine is to the left of the main altar. It contains a picture of the saint. Further to the left is the door to the shrine. The Stations of the Cross lined up around the floor gives it a temporary look. There is a portable statue of St. Peregrine healing a sick man and a glass-enclosed St. Peregrine carved in wood at Saint-Jean-Port-Joli. There is a reliquary here and some display cases containing objects dealing with the life and work of St. Peregrine.

To Help You Plan Your Pilgrimage

Schedule: The shrine is open all year, with pilgrimage season from May to September. The first Sunday of May is St. Peregrine's Day. The Feast of the Assumption (August 15), the anniversary of the birth of St. Peregrine (August 25), the Feast of the Birth of Mary (September 8) and the Feast of the Immaculate Conception (December 8) are also celebrated with pilgrimages.

A perpetual novena continues every Sunday morning all year. In early March a novena begins in preparation for the Feast of St. Peregrine and continues each Sunday afternoon until May. In early May there is an evening triduum in preparation for the Feast of St. Peregrine. The feast day begins in the afternoon with Adoration of the Sacrament, Blessing of the Sick, a Mass and procession in the streets.

On Good Friday a Way of the Cross begins early in the morning at St. Clement's Church, stops at 12 other churches and ends at St. Eusèbe in the afternoon.

For your convenience: The church is fully equipped for the handicapped. On feast days there are religious articles for sale.

For further information: The Work of St. Peregrine, 1850 Bercy Street, Suite 1011A, Montreal, QC H2K 2V2. ☎ (514) 525-9207; web site: www.makisost.net-peregrin.

Also of interest: The Shrine of the Holy Rosary and of St. Jude is not far west at St. Denis Street. (See next entry.)

Shrine of the Holy Rosary and of St. Jude

This shrine is on the busy thoroughfare of St. Denis Street, south of the intersection with Duluth Avenue.

St. Jude

*The popularity of St. Jude can be gauged by the many no-
tices of gratitude to this saint published in the personal sections
of our daily newspapers. St. Jude Thaddeus, one of the twelve
apostles, is credited with the Epistle of St. Jude in the New Testament. Devotion to St. Jude as the patron of hopeless cases
began in 18th-century Germany and France. Jude is also
honoured in the Orthodox and Eastern churches.*

The Rosary

The Rosary, a meditation on the mysteries of the entire Christian faith, developed from the 12th to the 15th centuries. It was
spread especially by the Dominicans and by Rosary confraternities. One tradition tells of the Virgin appearing to St. Dominic,
presenting him with a Rosary and asking him to preach it.

The Shrine

The Shrine of the Holy Rosary and of St. Jude was originally built in 1905 as the Irish parish of St. Agnes. In 1953 the
Dominicans bought it for a shrine.

The exterior of the dark grey stone church is in a heavy
Gothic style, but the interior is light and airy. The interior is
plain, except for the large and brilliant stained glass window in
the wall behind the main altar.

On the right side of the main altar is an arched niche holding a statue of St. Jude carved by Médard Bourgault. Nearby is
an unusually large stand of votive lights. On the left side of the
main altar in a niche is a grouping of the Virgin and Christ child
presenting the Rosary to St. Dominic and St. Catherine of Siena.

To Help You Plan Your Pilgrimage

Schedule: The church is open Monday to Saturday from 7:00
a.m. to 5:30 p.m., and Sunday from 7:30 a.m. to 5:30 p.m. The
Feast of St. Jude (October 28) is preceded by a novena. In the
fifth week of Lent there is another novena to St. Jude ending on
Palm Sunday.

The shrine has daily Masses, the morning one including
Lauds with the Dominican community. The Rosary is prayed
every afternoon except Sunday. There is a novena to St. Jude at
Masses every Tuesday and solemn novenas at the daily afternoon Mass.

Every February 18th there is a special Mass in honour of
the Blessed Fra Angelico, the famous Florentine painter who
was a Dominican. In addition there is an exhibition of the work

of local artists. At the beginning of the Montreal Jazz Festival each July, the Trio François Bourassa performs a Jazz Mass in the shrine. There are also four organ concerts per year.

For your convenience: Parking is available along the nearby streets. Washrooms and a religious articles shop are located in the parish house.

For further information: Shrine of the Holy Rosary and St. Jude, 3980 St. Denis Street, Montreal, QC H2W 2M3. ☎ (514) 845-0285; 🖳 (514) 845-3974.

Also of interest: The Jeanne Mance Centre and the Chapel at the Hotel Dieu are to the west, while the Shrine of Our Lady of Lourdes is south.

St. Joseph's Oratory

Sitting on the northwest slope of Mount Royal in the middle of Montreal, St. Joseph's Oratory is the largest shrine in Canada with over 2 million visitors per year. It is the largest shrine in the world dedicated to St. Joseph. Its dome is the third largest cupola in the world. It is the largest church in Canada. The cross on the dome is the highest point in the city of Montreal.

History

Despite its importance, St. Joseph's Oratory is not among the oldest shrines in Canada. Its founding and early development are closely tied up with the life of one man, Brother André (Frère André). Born Alfred Bessette in 1845, in the village of St-Grégoire d'Iberville, he was orphaned at age 11.

From his earliest years, Alfred had a great devotion to St. Joseph. In 1870, the same year that Pope Pius IX proclaimed Joseph patron of the universal church, Alfred entered the novitiate of the Congregation of Holy Cross in Montreal to become a brother, despite poor health and a lack of education.

As Brother André, he spent the next 40 years as doorkeeper at Notre Dame College.

Brother André often visited the sick; he would rub them with oil he took from a lamp that burned before the statue of St. Joseph in the college chapel. As word spread of physical healings, crowds of sick people began to come to the college, causing much embarrassment for Brother André and his superiors. The solution was to build a small chapel on land the college owned across the street on Mount Royal. As the hundreds of visitors became thousands, more and more additions were made to the chapel.

The suffering evident in the years before World War I convinced Brother André that the City of Montreal needed a symbol of God's love for the human race and he decided to build a shrine to St. Joseph. He and his supporters began a campaign and were able to raise enough money so that the cornerstone could be laid in 1916. The crypt was completed in 1918 and the upper church begun in 1924.

In his 70s and 80s Brother André travelled around raising money for the building and never lost confidence that it would be completed despite the economic depression. When he died in 1937 at the age of 91, over a million people filed past his coffin during a seven-day wake in the crypt church.

In 1967 the oratory was finally completed. In 1982 Brother André was declared "Blessed" by Pope John Paul II.

The Shrine

The main entrance to the shrine is on Queen Mary Road. In the middle of the pedestrian way up to the shrine is a monument with a statue of St. Joseph carrying the Christ child. Of the three staircases, the central is a Scala Sancta for pilgrims ascending on their knees.

The lower church or crypt has a seating capacity of 1,000. It has elaborately-sculpted lights and very fine plasterwork. Over the main altar is a 3-metre-high statue of St. Joseph carrying the Christ child. It was sculpted in white Carrara marble by Giacomini in 1917. The exterior of the upper church is in the Italian Renaissance style. The dome, made of poured cement covered with copper, was designed by French Benedictine Dom Paul Bellot.

The interior was designed by Canadian Gerard Notebaert. Everything seems to be on a gigantic scale here – from the seven-sided concrete arches to the abstract metal altar screen. The large crucifix behind the altar and the twelve apostles grouped in threes in the transepts, all sculpted by French artist Henri Charlier, serve to reinforce the dramatic austerity of this church. Some colour is provided by the mosaics in the sanctuary and by the stained glass windows in the walls and at the base of the dome.

The Blessed Sacrament Chapel is in the apse behind the altar screen. Large, round columns of green marble with gold mosaic capitals hold up a hemi-cycle ceiling covered in gold mosaic. As you leave the church, note the superb organ in the loft above the entrance.

All pilgrims to St. Joseph's will want to visit the votive chapel beside the crypt church. This high-ceilinged art deco hall is like no other room in Canada. Vigil lights, mostly red, are everywhere, even built into the decoration of the walls. On the walls hang many *ex-votos*, such as crutches left by grateful pilgrims. Near the centre is a large statue of St. Joseph with a fountain and a lamp rack containing 3,500 vigil lights.

To the right is a passageway that leads to Brother André's tomb. Near the west door of the votive chapel is a low tower hung with a carillon of bells once intended for Paris' Eiffel Tower. At the first exhibition level is a scale model of the oratory and photographs of the development of this shrine. The next level is the concourse hall, a good place to sit and relax for a few minutes. At this level are the Museum of Brother André, the roof terrace for viewing the city, and the door to the Way of the Cross on the mountainside.

The Stations are larger-than-life stone groups scattered through a wooded garden on the rocky mountain side. The best time to visit them is at night, when they are dramatically spot-lighted and you catch glimpses of the lighted city below. On evenings through July and August, the Mount Royal Players perform a play on the Passion of Christ along the Way of the Cross.

The final exhibition level has a permanent exhibition on St. Joseph, including an art and wax museum. From November to February there is a spectacular exhibition of Christmas cribs from over 60 countries.

Brother André's original chapel of 1904 and his room still exist. To reach them you must go out the door of the west transept of the upper church and follow the path.

To Help You Plan Your Pilgrimage

Schedule: The shrine is open all year from 7:00 a.m. to 10:00 p.m. From March 10 to 18, there is a novena for the Feast of St. Joseph (March 19). The Feast of St. Joseph the Worker is celebrated on May 1. From August 1 to 9, there is the novena in honour of Brother André. On August 9, the celebration of Brother André's birthday includes a candlelight procession. On the last Sunday of August an annual pilgrimage leaves the shrine for St-Grégoire d'Iberville, the birthplace of Brother André. Once a month there is a Mass of remembrance for families who have recently lost a member. Schedules are available for open air theatre, organ recitals and carillon concerts.

For your convenience: The shrine is fully equipped. There are a general pilgrim's hostel and a pavilion for the sick and handicapped on the grounds, a shuttle-bus from the main gate to the shrine, spiritual counselling, guided tours, a gift shop and a bookstore.

For further information: St. Joseph's Oratory, 3800 Queen Mary Road, Montreal, QC H3V 1H6. ☎ (514) 733-8211; 🖷 (415) 733-9735; e-mail: pelerinage@osj.qc.ca; web site: www.saint-joseph.org. *The Oratory Magazine* and its French edition, *L'Oratoire*, keep you in touch with events at the Oratory.

Also of interest: Not far away is the largest illuminated cross in the world on Mount Royal, and the Marie-Rose Centre. (See separate entry.)

Tomb of St. Marguerite Bourgeoys

The tomb is at the Marguerite Bourgeoys Centre in the Motherhouse of the Congregation of Notre Dame at 4877 Westmount Avenue. Take Sherbrooke west to Claremont and then head north to Westmount Avenue. Enter by the west door.

Marguerite Bourgeoys

Marguerite Bourgeoys was born in 1620 in Troyes, France. In 1640 she experienced a religious conversion during a Marian procession and began to work with an association of young women preparing to teach children of the poor. The director of this association happened to be the sister of the Sieur de Maisonneuve who founded the city of Montreal (Ville-Marie) in 1642. The colony needed teachers and Marguerite volunteered to take the arduous voyage across the Atlantic in 1653.

In 1658 she began the first school in Montreal and formed the basis of her new Congregation of Notre Dame, one of the earliest uncloistered communities in the Church. In 1668 she started La Providence, a vocational school for household arts (now the St. Gabriel Museum) in Point St. Charles.

In the last years of her life Marguerite finished an autobiography or spiritual testament. She died on January 12, 1700. Since then, devotion to Mother Bourgeoys has grown and she has been credited with several miracles. She was canonized by Pope John Paul II in 1982 in Rome.

Today her 2,300 sisters work in education and various social and family ministries, not only in Canada but in several countries of Asia and Latin America. In 1981 the Congregation came full circle when Marguerite's sisters began work in Troyes, France, her birthplace.

The Centre

Near the entrance is a museum displaying some of Marguerite's personal belongings, an original portrait of her and documents of her time. Across the hall is an audio-visual presentation of her life. (Arrangements should be made in advance.) Next to this is a religious articles stand.

The chapel is on the floor above. It is restrained in decoration but very beautiful. The tan-coloured marble tomb is in the middle of the sanctuary. On the back wall of the sanctuary is a large crucifix with a bronze corpus surrounded by eight tiny windows of stained glass. To the right is a mural of Marguerite Bourgeoys with two children. Beneath the railing of the choirloft is a series of paintings on her life. The Stations of the Cross are in mosaic of the highest quality.

To Help You Plan Your Pilgrimage

Schedule: Mass may be celebrated on the tomb itself for groups that bring their own priest. Arrangements should be made in advance. The Feast of St. Marguerite Bourgeoys (January 12) is celebrated in a different church in Montreal every year.

The centre is open from 10:00 a.m. to 5:00 p.m. from May 1 to October 31; is open from 11:00 a.m. to 3:30 p.m. from November 1 to January 15 and from March 15 to April 30; and is closed from January 16 to March 14 except for Sunday Mass. Tours are available in English or French.

For your convenience: The centre is equipped for the handicapped.

For further information: Marguerite Bourgeoys Centre, Congregation of Notre Dame, 4877 Westmount Avenue, Montreal, QC H3Y 1X9. phone (514) 282-8670, ext. 221; ▤ (514) 282-8672; e-mail: museemb@globetrotter.net; web site: www.marguerite-bourgeoys.com.

Also of interest: Other places associated with Marguerite Bourgeoys include St. Gabriel Museum (2146 Favard Street, Point St. Charles, Montreal) and Church of Notre-Dame-de-Bon-Secours in Old Montreal. (See separate entry.)

Tomb of St. Marguerite d'Youville

This is the tomb of the founder of the Grey Nuns, the first saint actually born in Canada. Part of the Motherhouse of the Grey Nuns, an old landmark in the centre of Montreal, the Marguerite d'Youville Centre has its entrance at 1185 St. Mathieu Street, around the corner from St. Catherine Street.

Quebec

The Centre

Ring the bell and you will be admitted and taken on a tour of the Motherhouse. The approach is mainly historical. If you are alert you will receive insights into the life and times of Marguerite d'Youville in 18th-century Canada and into the work of her order.

In 1747 the Grey Nuns began administering the General Hospital in Old Montreal. It was only in 1871 that they moved their Motherhouse to the corner of Guy and St. Mathieu. The chapel, with room for over 1,000 worshippers, was opened in 1878. The style is Romanesque. The altars of the semi-rotundas and the holy water fonts come from the original Motherhouse. The statue of Marguerite was placed in the sanctuary when she was beatified in 1959. If you look high up near the vaults of the nave of the chapel, you will see two Romanesque arched galleries. Here, out of sight of the congregation, the retired and infirm sisters sit during Mass.

Down in the crypt of the church is a graveyard where until the year 1896 the Grey Nuns were buried. The birth-death dates on the crosses show that many of them died young, usually of tuberculosis from working in the swampy area of old Montreal down by the river. The re-created bedroom and office of Marguerite d'Youville are here with the original ceilings, floors and furnishings. The tour through the Motherhouse brings you past several other reconstructed rooms and a small museum.

The Shrine of Marguerite d'Youville was set up after her beatification in 1959. In the sanctuary of this chapel is the tomb. It consists of an altar in rich brown onyx, with a glass window displaying a life-size wax figure of a recumbent St. Marguerite. At the base of the altar are the concrete-enclosed remains of the saint.

To Help You Plan Your Pilgrimage

Schedule: The centre is open Tuesday to Sunday from 1:30 to 4:00 p.m. Tours are available in either English or French. Groups should make advance reservations. There are novenas in the shrine every afternoon and Masses in the community chapel every morning. There is a religious articles shop here.

For further information: Marguerite d'Youville Centre, 1185 St. Mathieu Street, Montreal, QC H3H 2H6. ☎ (514) 932-7724; 🖳 (514) 932-7851; e-mail: centremdy@mmsgm.qc.ca.

Also of interest: Other places associated with Marguerite d'Youville include the old house where she lived at 138 Saint-Pierre Street in Old Montreal, by the waterfront. It has been restored but is not open to the public. Varennes, across the river, has the Shrine of St. Marguerite d'Youville. (See separate entry.)

NEUVILLE

Processional Chapel

Neuville is just west of Quebec City on Highway 138. Behind the Church of St-François de Sales is a beautiful stone processional chapel. Built in 1735 with a slender spire, it is a good example of the type of chapel that was the destination of the procession of Corpus Christi (now the Feast of the Body and Blood of Christ – the Thursday after Holy Trinity). The Corpus Christi Mass would have been celebrated here. The parish church has an 18th-century baldachino, three altars by François Baillairgé and 21 paintings by Antoine Plamondon.

NOTRE-DAME-DE-LA-SALETTE

Shrine of Notre-Dame-de-La-Salette

The village is in the Outaouais region of Quebec. From Hull take Highway 50 to Buckingham and then Highway 309 north.

History

In 1846 Mary appeared to two peasant children at La Salette, an isolated spot in the mountains of southeastern France. The message of La Salette that she confided to the children was the need for penance. Exactly 40 years later, in 1886, the Outaouais shrine was erected.

The Shrine

Today the shrine is on the main street of the village. The lower part consists of an open grassy area with a tiny wooden shrine whose doors open outward on pilgrimage day. The upper part, with the same arrangement, sits on top of a rock. Joining the two parts is a dramatic staircase of over 200 steps up the side of a cliff. The Stations of the Cross follow the staircase.

At the top is a statue of Our Lady of La Salette and a large wooden cross that is illuminated at night. At the top is a magnificent view of the valley of the Lièvre River.

To Help You Plan Your Pilgrimage

Schedule: The one pilgrimage day is the second or third Sunday in September. On that day Mass is celebrated both on top of the rock and at the foot of the rock for those who cannot climb. There is a Blessing of the Sick. The pilgrimage is largely a parish affair and there is a community meal afterwards at the church. The shrine is open year round, but is less accessible in winter due to snow.

For your convenience: There is a hotel in the village and plenty of camping spots nearby.

For further information: Notre-Dame-de-La-Salette Parish, Notre-Dame-de-La-Salette, QC J0X 2L0. ☎ (819) 986-3381 or (819) 766-2728; 🖳 (819) 766-2781; rayberub@attcanada.ca.

Also of interest: The shrine at Mayo is not far away. (See separate entry.)

NOTRE-DAME-DES-BOIS

Chapel of Saint-Joseph-de-la-Montagne

The village of Notre-Dame-des-Bois is about 70 kilometres east of Sherbrooke. Take Highway 108 to Cookshire and turn onto Highway 212 to Notre-Dame.

History

In the centre of the village and in front of the parish church is a large rock with a shrine of the Virgin Mary. Carved on the rock is the date June 17, 1875 – the year that the area was first opened for settlement. Bishop Racine of Sherbrooke had told the settlers to look for a place that had a good water supply. On June 17 they found a good place for a village in the middle of the woods and they began to argue about the best place to look for a spring. What seemed to be a pile of debris covered in moss drew their attention. When they cleared away the plants they found the rock and a spring flowing from its base. Here they began building the village of Notre-Dame-des-Bois (Our Lady of the Woods).

The Shrine
The local Shrine of Saint-Joseph-de-la-Montagne is on the
summit of Mt. Megantic to the northwest of the village. The
shrine began around 1882 with popular devotions in the face
of violent windstorms that were destroying the crops. The
present chapel was built in 1913.

To Help You Plan Your Pilgrimage

Schedule: There is Mass here every Sunday afternoon throughout July and until the Feast of the Assumption (August 15).

For your convenience: There are accommodations in the village.

For further information: Notre-Dame-des-Bois Parish, 25 Côte de
l'Église, Notre-Dame-des-Bois, QC J0B 2E0. ☎ (819) 888-2292.

Also of interest: The parish church, built in 1954, is interesting.
There is an observatory on top of Mt. Megantic.

OKA

Calvary
Oka is a village on Highway 344 west of Montreal.

The Stations of the Cross
*The devotion called the Stations of the Cross grew out of
the medieval pilgrimages to Jerusalem when pilgrims stopped
to pray at certain fixed points along the Via Dolorosa, the path
that Jesus is believed to have taken to Calvary. In the 14th century, when travel to the Holy Land became increasingly more
dangerous, replicas of the Way of the Cross became a popular
substitute in Europe.*

History
In 1740, Sulpician missionary Father Hamon Le Guen, a
native of Brittany where the Stations of the Cross devotions
were popular, initiated the construction of a Way of the Cross
on Oka Mountain. Between 1740 and 1742, the Indians built
the seven chapels out of local stone plastered with mortar.

The Sulpicians brought seven paintings of Christ's Passion
from France and placed them in the seven chapels. But because of the harsh climate the paintings began to deteriorate in
the unheated chapels and they were replaced in 1775 and 1776
with wooden bas-relief copies by Belleville.

At the beginning, the Indians from Oka, Kahnawake and Saint-Regis regularly came on pilgrimage in autumn before going on the hunt. But by the late 19th century, with the general revival of pilgrimages and the development of steamship and railway lines that made travel from Montreal easy, the Indians were soon outnumbered by outsiders. Angered by this and by land disputes with the Sulpicians, they stopped coming to the shrine.

In 1881 Trappist monks from France founded a monastery at Oka and eventually began to produce their famous Oka cheese. The Calvary reached the peak of its popularity in 1899, when over 30,000 pilgrims came for one feast day. Thereafter it began a long decline.

By the late 1960s the Calvary was no longer attracting many pilgrims and the chapels were allowed to fall into disrepair. In 1970 vandals broke into two of the chapels and partially destroyed two bas-reliefs. The outcry from history conservationists and heritage-minded people led the National Gallery of Canada to restore all the bas-reliefs and send them across Canada on exhibition.

The Calvary

The four white-washed oratories along the pathway through the woods have window-like openings (no doors) that reveal a scene of the Passion when their shutters are opened. The three chapels at the top of the mountain have doors. The central chapel with its Crucifixion scene is the only one big enough to admit a small group of pilgrims. Mass can be celebrated in this chapel.

Don't forget to drop in to the Church of the Annunciation in Oka to see the original Way of the Cross paintings. Also, the restored bas-reliefs are in the side chapel of Kateri Tekakwitha.

To Help You Plan Your Pilgrimage

Schedule: On the Sunday closest to the Feast of the Triumph of the Cross (September 14), reproductions of the bas-reliefs are placed in the chapels and oratories. Beginning in the early afternoon there is Mass in the parish church followed by a procession and Stations of the Cross on the mountain.

At the Trappist monastery there are daily evening Masses and a Sunday morning Mass. The daily Liturgy of the Hours is at 8:30 a.m., 11:40 a.m., 1:30 p.m., and 5:15 p.m.

For your convenience: There is parking available at the provincial recreation park. There are a few rooms reserved at the monastery for pilgrims, but you must book in advance. Write to Abbey of Notre-Dame-du-Lac, 1600 Oka Road, R.R. #1, Oka, QC J0N 1E0. ☎ (450) 479-8361. Montreal's hotels and motels are not far away.

For further information: Annunciation Parish, 181, rue des Anges, P.O. Box 177, Oka, QC J0N 1E0. ☎ (450) 479-8331; 🖷 (450) 479-8437; e-mail: info@paroisse-lannonciation.qc.ca; web site: http://www.paroisse-lannonciation.qc.ca. Radio-Canada produced a 24-minute film on the Oka Calvary, *La Fête du Calvaire*, in 1973.

Also of interest: Visit the chapel of the Trappist monastery. The shrine at Lachute is not far away. (See separate entry.)

PERCÉ

Statue of Ste. Anne

Percé is at the eastern tip of the Gaspé Peninsula. Take Highway 132.

In 1892 a huge statue of Ste. Anne, carved by Jean-Baptiste Côté, was placed at the top of Mont Sainte-Anne. In 1962 it was replaced by a replica. The trail to Mont Sainte-Anne begins behind the Church of St-Michel. The old statue of Ste. Anne can be seen in the parish church, dwarfing everything around it.

To Help You Plan Your Pilgrimage

Schedule: There is a local pilgrimage for the Feast of Ste. Anne (July 26).

Also of interest: St-Michel is an unusual example of Victorian Romanesque architecture in local red sandstone. It was at Percé that Bishop Laval celebrated his first Mass on Canadian soil in 1659. The famous Percé Rock is not to be missed.

POINTE-AU-PÈRE

Shrine of Ste. Anne

Pointe-au-Père is on the south shore of the St. Lawrence River, 10 kilometres northeast of Rimouski.

History

In the late 19th century, Pointe-au-Père was a stopover for ocean liners arriving in the St. Lawrence River. It was only natural that when the first wooden chapel was built in 1873 it should be named in honour of Ste. Anne, patroness of mariners. In 1875 a statue of Ste. Anne was donated; the pilgrimages began and soon became diocesan. In the late 1950s the brick church was replaced with a larger and more modern church in stone and concrete.

The Shrine

Today a statue of Ste. Anne stands on the gable of the church above the entranceway. Inside, to the right of the sanctuary is the large bronze statue of Ste. Anne from the older church. It is an exact copy of the one in the Shrine of Ste. Anne at Auray, Brittany, France. In front of the church is another statue of Ste. Anne that is part of a fountain. On the grounds is a statue of St. Joseph with the child Jesus, a statue of St. John Eudes, founder of the Eudists, a Calvary and a Lourdes grotto. Worth noting are the 18th-century British cannons by the Calvary.

To Help You Plan Your Pilgrimage

Schedule: The summer months, especially July and August, are pilgrimage season. The big day is the Feast of Ste. Anne (July 26), with a preparatory novena from July 17 to 25. During the novena there are confessions, devotions to Ste. Anne and Masses. On July 22 there is the gathering of the sick and handicapped with an anointing of the sick, devotions to Ste. Anne and Mass. On the Feast of Ste. Anne there are Masses, confessions and prayers to Ste. Anne.

For your convenience: There are motels and restaurants in the town of Pointe-au-Père and in Rimouski.

For further information: Pointe-au-Père Parish, 1095 du Parc, Pointe-au-Père, QC G5M 1M2.

Also of interest: In a small cemetery situated on rue du Fleuve are the graves of those drowned in the sinking of the ocean liner Empress of Ireland in 1914.

POINTE-NAVARRE

Shrine of Notre-Dame-des-Douleurs (Our Lady of Sorrows)

The shrine is only a few kilometres west of the Town of Gaspé on Highway 132, about 75 kilometres from Percé. At Pointe-Navarre a pilgrim has no doubt that the sea is near – the sign for the shrine is on the sail of a boat. The blue and white colours of the shrine are not only the colours of Mary but reminders of the sea. From the shrine one can see for miles along the beautiful Bay of Gaspé.

History

The history of the Shrine of Our Lady of Sorrows is largely the story of Father Jean-Marie Watier (1897–1968). Born at Ste-Anne-de-Bellevue, he studied at Rigaud and frequented the Shrine of Our Lady of Lourdes there. Ordained a Servite priest in 1928, he was asked to take over the Parish of St. Majorique in the Gaspé in 1938 and the next year he built a tiny mission church at Pointe-Navarre.

From the very beginning he showed an interest in setting up a shrine at Pointe-Navarre in honour of Our Lady of the Seven Sorrows. The building was finished in 1942 and in 1948 it was recognized as the national shrine to Our Lady of Sorrows. A man of deep faith and of prayer, Watier became known as a healer among the people of the Gaspé.

The Shrine

From the highway the first thing you notice is the statue of Mary on a pedestal and a long flight of steps leading to the white and blue church on the side of the hill. The interior of the church is simple and peaceful. Dominating the sanctuary is a large natural wood crucifix by Médard Bourgault. Also in the sanctuary is the statue of Our Lady of Sorrows, traditionally represented with seven swords piercing her heart. This was donated by pilgrims from Montreal.

The Stations of Our Lady of Sorrows in the church are in ceramic by Rose-Anne Monna. On the left is Médard Bourgault's representation of St. Joseph as an ordinary Quebec worker holding the child Jesus.

Outside, to the left of the church is the six-sided Memorial Chapel with the tomb of Father Watier. Behind the church is a landscaped terrace with a Grotto of Our Lady of Lourdes.

To the right of the terrace is a staircase that takes you up the mountain and through the trees. Here is an open-air altar for Mass and a grassy clearing that can accommodate over 1,000 people. At the opposite end of this clearing is a beautiful Calvary with the Virgin Mary, St. John and Mary Magdalene. Beyond this, higher up the mountain, are three hermitages or *poustinias* for solitary meditation.

The main path carries you to the right and to a field with the Way of Our Lady of Sorrows. This consists of stands holding very fine bronze plaques by French sculptor Grand'homme Andro. There is also a *Pietà* here. On the way back to the entrance to the grounds, notice the statue of St. Michael and the holy well. One of the shrine's three bells comes from a shipwreck and was later used to warn fishing boats during fog.

To Help You Plan Your Pilgrimage

Schedule: The shrine is open all year, but the season for group pilgrimages runs from May to the end of October. In summer the church is open from 6:30 a.m. to 8:30 p.m. The Feast of the Assumption is celebrated on August 15 and Our Lady of Sorrows on September 15.

For your convenience: The shrine is fully equipped and includes accommodations and food.

For further information: Shrine of Our Lady of Sorrows, 765 Pointe-Navarre Boulevard, Gaspé, QC G0C 1R0. ☎ (418) 368-

2133; 🖳 (418) 368-5465; e-mail: <u>sanctuai@globetrotter.qc.ca</u>; web site: <u>http://pages.infinit.net/servites</u>. The shrine produces its own Pilgrim's Manual, mostly in French, but with some prayers and hymns in English.

Also of interest: Across the Bay (take Highway 132) is the Church of St. Majorique with a beautiful Calvary in its cemetery. In front of Gaspé Cathedral is a 9-metre-high granite cross commemorating the wooden cross erected by Jacques Cartier in 1534. At Percé is the Mont Ste. Anne statue. (See separate entry.)

PORT-DANIEL

Calvary

Port-Daniel is on the southern shore of the Gaspé Peninsula where the Bay of Chaleur enters the Gulf of St. Lawrence. Take Highway 132. The Calvary group is near the church of Notre-Dame-du-Mont-Carmel. The crucifix was sculpted by Médard Bourgault.

QUEBEC CITY

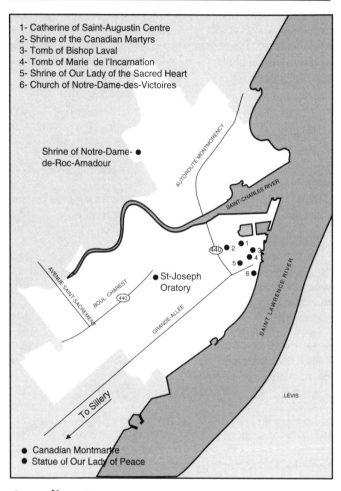

1- Catherine of Saint-Augustin Centre
2- Shrine of the Canadian Martyrs
3- Tomb of Bishop Laval
4- Tomb of Marie de l'Incarnation
5- Shrine of Our Lady of the Sacred Heart
6- Church of Notre-Dame-des-Victoires

Shrine of Notre-Dame-de-Roc-Amadour

AUTOROUTE MONTMORENCY

SAINT-CHARLES RIVER

440

St-Joseph Oratory

AVENUE SAINT-SACREMENT

BOUL. CHAREST

440

GRANDE-ALLÉE

SAINT LAWRENCE RIVER

To Sillery

LÉVIS

Canadian Montmartre
Statue of Our Lady of Peace

Canadian Montmartre
(Shrine of the Sacred Heart)

The Canadian Montmartre is situated on a 60-metre-high cliff overlooking the St. Lawrence River. The address is 1679 chemin Saint-Louis.

History

In 1917 Cardinal Bégin accepted the offer of Assumptionist Father Marie-Clément Staub that the Assumptionists move to the Quebec City area to set up an Archconfraternity of Prayer and Penitence of Montmartre and found a Shrine to the Sacred Heart of Jesus. It was completed in 1927. In 1953 the shrine was formally recognized by the Canadian bishops as the Canadian Montmartre.

The Shrine

The brown brick sanctuary has a bell-tower with a silver steeple. Inside, a statue of Jesus of the Sacred Heart stands with arms outstretched in a lighted niche high on the wall behind the altar table. It is surrounded by painted angels in clouds. This ensemble is a copy of the original at Paray-le-Monial where St. Margaret Mary lived.

In the middle of the grounds is the beautiful fountain of the Assumption of the Virgin Mary in the shape of a star with 15 points symbolizing the Mysteries of the Rosary. Pilgrim groups stand in a circle around the fountain to recite the Rosary.

The shrine's centre has an auditorium and chapel and facilities for meetings, conferences, retreats and rallies. Near it is an outdoor altar under two arches that form the letters IM for Immaculate Mary. This altar is used during the warm months. Under the trees is a marble and granite Stations of the Cross. Pilgrims are invited to visit the nearby Motherhouse of the Sisters of St. Joan of Arc and their shrines to St. Michael and Joan of Arc, Father Staub's Tomb, the old and the new chapels, a Lourdes grotto and a Calvary.

To Help You Plan Your Pilgrimage

Schedule: The shrine is open all year from 8:30 a.m. to 4:00 p.m. daily. Sometimes it stays open until 8:00 p.m. The Feast of the Sacred Heart is celebrated on the Friday following the second Sunday after Pentecost. A novena precedes it. In mid-June there is a blessing of the automobiles and, in mid-July, a day for the sick. The Feast of the Assumption (August 15) is preceded by a novena. Every Good Friday there is a Stations of the Cross pilgrimage on foot that begins at Notre Dame Basilica, proceeds to eight other churches, and ends at the Canadian Montmartre.

For your convenience: The shrine is fully equipped. There are accommodations on the grounds.

For further information: Canadian Montmartre, 1679 chemin St-Louis, Sillery, QC G1S 1G5. ☎ (418) 681-7357; 🖳 (418) 681-9644; e-mail: montmartre@videotron.ca; web site: http://pages.infinit.net/montmart. The shrine, along with the shrine at Beauvoir, produces a monthly review, *L'Appel du Sacré-Coeur.*

Also of interest: In front of the nearby Church of St-Michel is a huge statue of Mary Immaculate overlooking the river. (See separate entry.)

Catherine de Saint-Augustin Centre

The centre is in the northern end of the old walled city by the Hôtel-Dieu Hospital. The entrance is at 32 Charlevoix Street.

Catherine de Longpré

Catherine de Longpré was born in 1632 at Saint-Sauveur-le-Vicomte in Normandy, France. At an early age Catherine felt a call from God to religious life. When she was 12 she followed her older sister into an Augustinian convent and made her vows in 1646.

In 1639 the Augustinian sisters had been the first order to send missionaries to Canada. Catherine volunteered and in 1648, at the age of 16, sailed for Canada. The voyage took three months, during which time the plague broke out on the ship and many died. Catherine became afflicted with it but was strangely healed.

At Quebec she found plenty of work awaiting her. She learned a native Indian language and became an excellent nurse at the Hôtel-Dieu Hospital. In 1649 Huron refugees from Huronia began arriving in Quebec. The next winter there was famine at Quebec.

As troubles at Quebec mounted and the threat of Iroquois attacks increased, some sisters became discouraged and returned to France. But Catherine saw her vocation as one of staying in Canada. In May 1668, she caught an illness and, worn out with work, soon died. She had just turned 36.

Because she offered her life for the sake of the Church she is considered one of the founders of the Canadian Church. On April 23, 1989, she was beatified in Rome.

Today the Augustinian Sisters are united in a federation with headquarters in Sillery. They have many monasteries in Canada and missions in Paraguay and Haiti.

The Centre

Devotions to Catherine de Saint-Augustin began immediately with her death. Her bones were dug up in 1689, placed in a small casket and kept in the monastery. In 1717 artist Noël Levasseur produced a magnificent reliquary for the bones. In 1985, when the centre was founded, this reliquary became its focus. There is a slide show on her life and a museum.

To Help You Plan Your Pilgrimage

Schedule: The centre is open daily. Check the web site for details.

For further information: Catherine de Saint-Augustin Centre, 32 Charlevoix Street, Quebec, QC G1R 5C4. ☎ (418) 692-2492 ext. 240; 🖳 (418) 692-2668; e-mail: <u>centre.catherine@videotron.ca</u>; web site: <u>www.diocesequebec.qc.ca</u> (click on "Histoire").

Also of interest: The Hôtel-Dieu is the oldest hospital in North America. The church of the Hotel-Dieu was erected in 1800 and the interior decorated by Thomas Baillairgé. Pride of place goes to the little gilded statue of Our Lady of All Graces. Given to the church in 1737 by a man who had been saved from shipwreck after prayers to Mary, it has been venerated by the sick for over 250 years.

Church of Notre-Dame-des-Victoires

The church, on historic Place Royale in Lower Town, is the oldest church in Quebec City and one of the oldest shrines in Canada. The funicular from Upper Town is not far from here.

History

The church was founded by Bishops Laval and Saint-Vallier and built in 1688 on the spot where Champlain had constructed his house in 1608. It commemorates two French victories against the British invaders in 1690 and 1711. During the final siege of Quebec in 1759 the church was partially destroyed by the British batteries at Point-Lévis. It was restored in the 1760s and most recently in 1969. This was a special place of pilgrimage for sailors. The model of the ship Le Brezé that hangs from the ceiling of the church nave was given to the shrine by the Marquis de Tracy in thanksgiving for a safe voyage from France in 1664.

The Shrine

The church, facing Place Royale, is in a simple classical style with a triumphal arch over the entrance and two wheel windows on the facade. The retable of the main altar was done in a classical style by Raphaël Giroux between 1854 and 1857.

Above the tabernacle is the statue of Notre-Dame-des-Victoires carrying the child Jesus. Imported from France, the statue stands in a sunburst surrounded by many paintings and sculptures. A side chapel on the left has an altar and shrine dedicated to Ste. Geneviève.

To Help You Plan Your Pilgrimage

Schedule: Most of the visitors to the church today are tourists, but some pilgrims still come here. From May 1 to October 15 the church is open daily.

Saint-Joseph Oratory

The Oratory is in the convent of the Sisters of St. Joseph of St. Vallier. The convent was built in 1911 and the present chapel in 1925. The chapel has a series of paintings and stained glass windows on the life of St. Joseph.

To Help You Plan Your Pilgrimage

Schedule: The Oratory is open all year for private devotions but there are only local pilgrimages. The chapel is open from Monday to Saturday from 7:45 to 9:30 a.m., and Sunday from 8:00 a.m. to 12:00 p.m. The office is open Monday to Friday from 9:00 to 11:30 a.m. and from 1:30 to 4:00 p.m.

There is a small shop with religious articles relating to St. Joseph.

For further information: St. Joseph Oratory, 560 chemin Ste-Foy, Quebec, QC G1S 2J6. ☎ (418) 681-7361; ▤ (418) 683-4440.

Shrine of Notre-Dame de Roc-Amadour

The shrine is in the Church of St. Francis of Assisi on First Avenue, north of the St. Charles River.

History

This shrine has an association with the explorer Jacques Cartier. Cartier spent the winter of 1536 by the St. Charles River. So many of his crew died of scurvy that Cartier took an image of Notre-Dame de Roc-Amadour and placed it at the foot of a tree in the forest. He and his crew then marched, singing, in procession to the statue. Cartier vowed that if they were spared he would go in pilgrimage to the Shrine of  Notre-Dame de Roc-Amadour when he returned to France. Almost immediately, local Indians came and taught them how to make a natural remedy for scurvy.

When, in 1919, the Church of St. Francis of Assisi was built on this site, Cardinal Bégin set up a shrine to Notre-Dame de Roc-Amadour also. There is a statue here of the seated Virgin with the child Jesus on her lap holding the Gospels. Both are crowned. There is a relic of St. Amadour and many *ex-votos*.

To Help You Plan Your Pilgrimage

Schedule: The church is open Monday, Wednesday, Friday and Saturday from 2:30 to 5:00 p.m. The local pilgrimage is on the Feast of the Birth of Mary (September 8). On the Saturday night following the feast, a candlelight procession is made from Jacques Cartier's cross to the shrine.

For further information: Notre-Dame de Roc-Amadour Parish, 1400 Avenue François 1ᵉʳ, Quebec, QC G1L 4L2; ☎ (418) 525-7381 or (418) 523-8992 (parish); 🖳 (418) 529-5413.

Shrine of Our Lady of the Sacred Heart

The Shrine of Our Lady of the Sacred Heart is within the old walled city of Quebec at 71 Ste-Ursule Street.

History

This little masterpiece was built in 1909–1910 by F.-X. Berlinguet and Alphonse Laberge. Made of local greyish-brown stone, it is in the Gothic style, which is unusual among French Canadians. The reason that it is Gothic is that it is a replica of the Shrine of Our Lady of the Sacred Heart in Issoudun, France, the place where this devotion and the Missionaries of the Sacred Heart originated.

The Society of the Missionaries of the Sacred Heart was founded in Issoudun in 1854 by Father Jules Chevalier to renew the faith in France through devotion to the Sacred Heart. The Society originally was neither missionary nor international, but government persecution forced its members to leave France and find refuge in many countries around the world.

The Shrine

The facade of the shrine has two short spires rising from it. The facade wall includes four pointed-arch windows and a rose window. The interior is extremely beautiful, mainly due to the fine proportions of the pillars and the vaults. The walls of the nave are almost completely covered in *ex-voto* plaques right up to the vaults. The haut-relief Stations of the Cross have Gothic frames and the stained glass windows have interesting tracery. One window in the nave shows Jesus of the Sacred Heart appearing to St. Margaret Mary Alacoque.

Above the tabernacle in the sanctuary is the statue of Our Lady of the Sacred Heart. Both mother and child are crowned, and Mary's halo is lighted, as is the crescent moon at her feet. In the right side of the church you will find a long chapel, modern and plain, called the Chapel of Lights.

To Help You Plan Your Pilgrimage

Schedule: The shrine is open all year from 7:00 a.m. to 8:00 p.m. daily. There are daily and Sunday Masses.

For further information: Notre-Dame-du-Sacré-Coeur Shrine, 71 Ste-Ursule Street, P.O. Box 487, Haute-ville, Quebec, QC G1R 4R8. ☎ (418) 692-3787.

Shrine of the Canadian Martyrs

The shrine is at the corner of Dauphine Street and Auteuil Street within the walls of the old city.

History

The chapel originated with a lay Marian devotional group founded by the Jesuits in Quebec City in 1657. In 1803 this group received permission from the bishop to build a chapel of its own. In 1930 the whole exterior was changed. The interior has a carved and gilded high altar, several large oil paintings, sculptures by Pierre-Noël Levasseur and Alfred Laliberté and a Stations of the Cross by Médard Bourgault.

The chapel remained a Marian shrine until 1925. In that year the Canadian Martyrs were beatified in Rome and the Jesuits transformed the chapel into a shrine to them.

To Help You Plan Your Pilgrimage

Schedule: Today the shrine celebrates the Feast of the Canadian Martyrs (October 19), which is preceded by a special novena. The shrine has relics of three of the martyrs – Jean de Brébeuf, Charles Garnier and Gabriel Lalemant. It is open daily and on Sunday mornings.

For further information: Shrine of the Canadian Martyrs, 20 Dauphine Street, P.O. Box 188, Haute-ville, QC G1R 4P3. ☎ (418) 694-9616; 🖷 (418) 692-4662.

Statue of Our Lady of Peace

This huge statue of Mary Immaculate stands on Pointe-à-Puiseaux in front of the historic Church of St-Michel and overlooks the St. Lawrence River Valley.

The idea to build a statue to celebrate the role of Mary in evangelization and to commemorate the visit of Pope John Paul II to Canada arose among a group of laity in Quebec City in early 1984. These men and women found a site, collected money and commissioned sculptor Lewis Pagé to carve the figure in granite. The finished monument was blessed by Cardinal Vachon in October 1984. The statue is illuminated at night.

The Church of St-Michel, with its tall Gothic steeple, was built in 1858. Inside is the icon of Mary, Gate of Heaven.

To Help You Plan Your Pilgrimage

Schedule: The Church of St-Michel is open every day; call ahead for details. In the months of May and October there is a Mass every evening followed by the Rosary for groups of pilgrims. Every Marian feast day is celebrated with a solemn Mass that is preceded by 24 hours of Marian prayers.

For further information: Statue of Our Lady of Peace Foundation, 1600 Persico Street, Sillery (Quebec), QC G1T 1H3. ☎ (418) 527-3390; 🖷 (418) 527-8454. The Foundation produces a bulletin, *Fondation de la Statue de l'Immaculée.*

Tomb of Bishop Laval

In the fall of 1993 the remains of Bishop Laval were moved from the mortuary chapel in the seminary chapel (at the corner of Ste. Famille Street and de la Fabrique Street) to an apse-like shrine in the Basilica of Notre-Dame (Buade Street).

Bishop Laval

A very generous and holy man, Canada's first bishop was able to steer the Church around the shoals of political intrigue and provide a milieu in which extraordinary people such as Marie de l'Incarnation and Kateri Tekakwitha could flourish and the shrine at Ste. Anne de Beaupré could grow. Perhaps his greatest gift was the Seminary of Quebec, which made the local Church in Canada independent enough of the Church in France that it was able to survive the English conquest in the 18th century and go on to a renaissance in the 19th. Bishop Laval died in 1708 and was beatified in 1980.

The Shrine

The shrine is to the right of the nave. On a table-like stand is the bronze reclining figure of Laval in full vestments with a mitre and crook. Etched into the black stone floor is a map of New France. The street side of the shrine is also worth a visit.

The Basilica of Notre-Dame was begun in 1647 and was partly destroyed in the 1759 British siege of Quebec. In 1922 a fire destroyed much of the interior. The present Baroque interior, copying the earlier decoration, is one of the finest church interiors in the country. Opposite Bishop Laval's Tomb is a Sacred Heart Shrine, and the side altars, dedicated to St. Ann and the Holy Family, have both been built as shrines for fraternities. The tombs of the other bishops of Quebec are in the crypt. There are guided tours of both basilica and seminary.

Tomb of Marie de l'Incarnation

The Marie de l'Incarnation Centre is in the old Ursuline Convent at 10 Donnacona Street.

Marie de l'Incarnation

Marie Guyart was born in 1599 at Tours, France. At the age of 17 she married but within three years was left a widow with one son (who would later become a Benedictine). At this time in her life Marie decided not to remarry. She began to have mystical experiences and, at the age of 32, she joined the Ursuline Sisters. Stirred by her reading of the Jesuit Relations, she came to understand that her calling was that of a missionary to Canada.

Marie found a benefactress in Madame de la Peltrie, who had decided to devote her wealth to help establish the Ursuline Sisters in Canada. In 1639 they, and two other Ursulines, set sail for Canada. At Quebec Marie became the first superior of the Ursuline Convent. Now 40, she was living in a miserable hut for a convent in Lower Town and preparing to learn native languages and teach young Indian girls.

Within a few years she had built a new stone convent in Upper Town. When it burned in 1650 she built it anew. At the same time she ran a school for both French and Indian children, wrote treatises on theology and spirituality, compiled the first dictionaries in Algonquin and Iroquois, wrote her second autobiography, learned five native languages and translated a French catechism into Iroquois.

Having given her best years to help found the Church in Canada, Marie resigned her post as superior of the Ursulines at the age of 70. Her last three years were ones of ever-deepening mysticism and she died in 1672. On June 22, 1980, she was beatified in Rome by Pope John Paul II.

The Shrine

Three parts of the Ursuline Convent are accessible to visitors: the Ursuline Chapel, the Marie de l'Incarnation Centre and the Ursuline Museum.

The Ursuline Chapel is a 1902 copy of the 1723 chapel and the fourth chapel on this spot. Most of the interior furnishings, notably furniture by Pierre-Nöel Levasseur, come from the 1723 chapel. There are many art works here, including old masters made homeless at the time of the French Revolution. There is a plaque marking the grave of General Montcalm.

Beside the Ursuline Chapel is a small oratory with the tomb in dark stone. Groups bringing their own priest may arrange in advance for the celebration of Mass here.

The Marie de l'Incarnation Centre has a display of videos and objects relating to Marie de l'Incarnation, including her Rosary and a death mask.

The Ursuline Museum covers the work of the Ursuline Sisters during the 120 years they operated under the French Regime (1639–1759).

To Help You Plan Your Pilgrimage

Schedule: The Ursuline Convent is open from May to November. The chapel is open every day except Monday. The centre is open every day except Sunday morning and Monday. The museum hours are 9:30 a.m. to noon and 1:30 to 4:45 p.m. daily except Mondays. Sunday hours are 12:30 to 5:15 p.m.

For your convenience: There is parking at City Hall. There are washrooms at the shrine. The chapel and centre are accessible to the handicapped but the museum is not.

For further information: Director – Marie de l'Incarnation Centre, 10 Donnacona Street, Quebec, QC G1R 4T1.

RESTIGOUCHE

Shrine of Ste-Anne-de-Restigouche

The shrine, also called Ste-Anne-des-Micmacs, is on the Micmac Reservation of Restigouche on the north shore of the Bay of Chaleur in the Gaspé Peninsula. Restigouche, on Highway 132, faces Campbellton, New Brunswick, across the Bay.

History

In 1610, Membertou, the high chief of the Micmac, was baptized by the Récollet Fathers and the whole tribe soon followed. The Récollets were especially devoted to Ste. Anne and the Micmac became fond of the grandmother of Christ.

In 1760 the English defeated the French in the naval Battle of Restigouche and thereby gained control over the whole region. They began deporting the Acadian settlers, including the Récollets. The Micmac were left on their own but their faith never wavered. Their chapel burned down in 1790 but they replaced it. In 1845 Restigouche became the Parish of Ste-Anne-de-Restigouche and in 1894 the Capuchin Order arrived to direct the shrine.

The Shrine

The present parish church, built in 1926, is the seventh church on the spot. It has a tall bell-tower. In front of it is a monument to Chief Membertou erected in 1910. Inside the church are many paintings. The walls of the apse have arched panels of several saints. Over the tabernacle of the high altar is a painting of Ste. Anne with the child Mary.

To the left of the sanctuary is the statue of Ste. Anne with an arch of lights over her. In the right hand side of the church is Jacques Bourgault's sculpture of Blessed Kateri Tekakwitha, donated in memory of an Indian rights champion, Alphonse Metallic. In the cemetery by the church is a beautiful Calvary group.

To Help You Plan Your Pilgrimage

Schedule: The shrine is open all year on Tuesday to Friday from 9:00 to 11:00 a.m. and from 2:00 to 4:00 p.m., but the big pilgrimage day is the Feast of Ste. Anne (July 26). The relic of Ste. Anne is exposed for veneration for the whole of July and there is a novena to St. Anne from July 17 to 26. There are Masses throughout the feast day, the second-last one being for the sick. There are outdoor games, a salmon dinner around noon, and bingo in the evening.

For further information: Capuchin Order, P.O. Box 70, Pointe-à-la-Croix, QC G0C 1L0. ☎ (418) 788-2853; 🖳 (418) 788-2038.

Also of interest: Pointe-à-la-Croix is considered an historic site.

RIGAUD

Shrine of Our Lady of Lourdes

Rigaud is 35 kilometres west of Montreal by Highway 40. From the highway you can catch a glimpse of the shrine buildings among the trees on the slope of Rigaud Mountain. Cross the bridge. Turn right either at the light at the church or the light just beyond the church and follow the signs to the shrine. This is the most important shrine to Our Lady of Lourdes in Canada and receives about 125,000 pilgrims per year.

Lourdes

On February 11, 1858, Bernadette Soubirous, a 14-year-old peasant girl searching for firewood, had a vision of a woman in a hillside grotto near Lourdes, France. Bernadette returned 17 more times. On one occasion the woman caused a spring to gush up. During the 16th apparition the woman identified herself as Mary, the Immaculate Conception. Since then, Lourdes has become famous for its physical cures (and the source of much controversy in the medical field).

History

Just 16 years after the apparitions at Lourdes, France, the shrine at Rigaud was begun. The year was 1874 and Brother Ludger Pauzé, on the staff of Rigaud's Bourget College, decided to spread devotion to Our Lady of Lourdes in the region. He dug a small niche in a rock on Rigaud mountain and in it placed a 10-inch statue of Our Lady of Lourdes. As interest grew, the local parish donated the land that would allow the public to reach the shrine.

In 1886 the townspeople brought a large new statue of the Virgin and a figure of the kneeling Bernadette. In 1887 a domed eight-sided chapel was built on the highest point on the rock just above the grotto. By 1890 the railway line between Montreal and Ottawa was completed and the number of pilgrims grew.

During the 1930s many religious spectacles were presented at the shrine. The 1954 Marian Year, marking the centennial of the Dogma of the Immaculate Conception, was celebrated with the building of a new outdoor chapel near the base of the cliff. The year 1974 marked the centennial of the shrine and the installation of a Sound and Light Festival.

The Shrine

The flat, open ground in front of the rock is sometimes called the open-air cathedral or the *cathédrale de verdure* because of all the trees around it. There are pews or benches for over 3,000 people here. Directly in front of this is a raised terrace, beautifully landscaped, and the new stone chapel. Seen through a Gothic arch is the altar and the crowned statue of Our Lady of Rigaud in a niche. To the left is an enclosed annex with pews. There are many *ex-voto* plaques on the wall.

On the right-hand side of the terrace is the Grotto of Our Lady of Lourdes with many vigil lights. Under the trees is a simple Way of the Cross, a Grotto to the Sacred Heart of Jesus and a statue of Our Lady of Grace. The old domed chapel on top of the rock can be reached by flights of stone steps. Inside it is a carved wooden altar containing a statue of Our Lady of Lourdes. From the lookout there is a fine view of the town of Rigaud and the surrounding countryside.

To the right of the domed chapel is a path to a field called the Devil's Garden, a moraine that has been explained with an old legend of the Devil. There is a road to the top of Rigaud Mountain and a large iron cross that is illuminated at night.

To Help You Plan Your Pilgrimage

Schedule: The grounds are open from May 1 to September 30. The Feast of the Assumption is celebrated on August 15, with a triduum preceding it. For schedules of Masses, Benediction, Way of the Cross, and candlelight processions, please write.

For your convenience: The shrine is fully equipped. There are motels in Rigaud, Ste. Marthe, Hawkesbury and Dorion. There is a camping site east of Rigaud.

For further information: Our Lady of Lourdes Shrine, P.O. Box 158, Rigaud, QC J0P 1P0. To keep you up-to-date on shrine events, the shrine produces a yearly magazine in French, English and Italian.

Also of interest: An interesting Way of the Cross can be found at the cemetery at Rigaud. The Church of Ste. Madeleine is worth a visit. Oka has a Calvary and Lachute has a shrine. (See separate entries.)

ROQUEMAURE

Sainte-Anne-de-Roquemaure

Roquemaure is in northwestern Quebec, near Lake Abitibi and the Ontario border. From Rouyn-Noranda, take Highway 101 north just past Reneault. Turn left onto Highway 393. Follow it as it turns north until you come to the fourth crossing. Turn right and pass through Gallichan to Roquemaure.

The first pilgrimage was organized in 1939 through the influence of priests from Ste-Anne-de-la-Pocatière. The Church of Ste. Anne is the centre of the pilgrimage.

This pilgrimage is diocesan and usually lasts two days around the Feast of Ste. Anne (July 26). Usually there is Mass, Benediction and a blessing of religious articles.

SABREVOIS

Sainte-Anne-de-Sabrevois

Sabrevois is southeast of Montreal on the Richelieu River. From Montreal take Highway 10 east and then Highway 133 south.

In the Church of Ste. Anne is a statue and a relic of the grandmother of Christ. Both the Feast of Ste. Anne (July 26) and the Solemnity of Ste. Anne (the following Sunday) are celebrated. There is a Mass and a candlelight procession both evenings.

Also of interest: Just east of the town of Iberville is St-Grégoire, where Brother André was born. There is a monument to him there.

SAINT-BENOÎT-DU-LAC

Abbey of St-Benoît

Saint-Benoît-du-Lac is on Lake Memphrémagog, about 45 kilometres southwest of Sherbrooke.

History

The Benedictine monks from the Abbey of St. Wandrille in Normandy first came to Canada as refugees from an anti-clerical French government. With the help of the bishop of Sherbrooke they were able to buy a property on the shores of Lake Memphrémagog and inaugurate their new monastery in 1912. The monastery officially became an abbey in 1952.

The Abbey

The Abbey of St-Benoît is notable for its architecture. It was constructed during the 1930s to 1950s of different kinds of stone and brick. It was modified according to the plans of Dom Paul Bellot, who came from the famous Abbey of Solesmes in France. Bellot had designed the dome of St. Joseph's Oratory in Montreal, and at the Abbey he designed the tower of St. John the Baptist with a remarkable winding staircase. A relic of St. Benedict is kept in this tower.

The main church, designed by Dan Hanganu, has a stained glass window donated by the government of France. On the grounds are a farm, a building where cheese is made, and a shop with local products and religious articles made in European monasteries.

To Help You Plan Your Pilgrimage

Schedule: The abbey is open all year. The chapel is open daily. Retreatants and the general public may join in the Liturgy of the Hours with the monks: Matins at 5:00 a.m., Lauds at 7:30 a.m., Vespers at 5:00 p.m., and Compline at 7:45 p.m. Daily Mass is at 11:00 a.m. Confessions and consultation are available.

Every year, usually the last week of September or the first week of October, organized pilgrimages from several Canadian universities come to St-Benoît. The students come in buses, get off at places such as Austin and walk to the Abbey. Usually there is Mass and a lunch at the Abbey.

For your convenience: There is a hostel for men in the Abbey: ☎ (819) 843-4080. On the grounds is a hostel for women, the Villa Sainte-Scholastique: ☎ (819) 843-2340.

For further information: Write to Abbey of St-Benoît, Saint-Benoît-du-Lac, QC J0B 2M0.

Also of interest: There are shrines at Sherbrooke, Beauvoir and Ste-Anne-de-la-Rochelle. (See separate entries.) Every summer at Mont Orford there is a youth music festival.

SAINT-CÉLESTIN

Calvary
Saint-Célestin is southeast of Trois-Rivières on the south side of the St. Lawrence River on Highway 155. It has an eight-figure Calvary erected in 1932.

Nicolet, with its unusual cathedral, is not far away.

SAINT-ÉLIE

Calvary
Saint-Élie is about 55 kilometres northwest of Trois-Rivières on Highway 351.

The Calvary was first erected in 1896 by Father Frédéric Janssoone and has been recently restored. The Stations of the Cross are on the side of a hill. There is a local pilgrimage on the Feast of the Triumph of the Cross (September 14). There is also a statue of the Virgin here and a devotion to Our Lady of Perpetual Help.

The shrine is open all summer.

SAINT-EMOND-DE-GRANTHAM

Grotto of Our Lady of Lourdes
Saint-Emond is about 45 kilometres west of Drummondville, just off Highway 122. There is no pilgrimage but there are occasional Masses at the grotto during the warm weather.

SAINT-FABIEN-SUR-MER

Shrine of Notre-Dame-des-Murailles

Saint-Fabien-sur-Mer is on the south shore of the St. Lawrence River, 30 kilometres southeast of Rimouski on Highway 132. It is just north of Saint-Fabien.

The Grotto of Our Lady of Lourdes was erected in 1923 by a member of the Martin family as a result of a vow made for a safe return from Europe to Canada in 1914.

The shrine, on the cliff by the river, is open from St-Jean-Baptiste Day (June 24) to Labour Day (first Monday in September). There is no special pilgrimage day. In addition to the grotto there are a stone altar, a chapel and a spring.

SAINT-GÉRARD

Shrine of St. Gerard

Saint-Gérard is about 60 kilometres northeast of Sherbrooke on Highway 112.

St. Gerard Majella

St. Gerard Majella was born in 1726 near Naples, Italy. It is said that when he was a tiny child playing at the Sanctuary of Capotignano, the Infant Jesus left the Madonna's arms and came down to play with him. As a Redemptorist brother he became known for his healings of the sick. He died in 1755 at the age of 29 and was canonized in 1904. He is the patron saint of children and of mothers, especially expectant mothers.

The parish was founded in 1905 and named by Bishop Paul LaRocque, who had recently come from the canonization of St. Gerard in Rome. The pilgrimage to St. Gerard was encouraged by parish priest Canon Charles-Joseph Roy and he collected several relics of St. Gerard.

The Shrine

The brick Church of St. Gerard is relatively plain on the outside, with arched windows and a small wheel window over the door. At a back corner of the church is a low and odd-shaped bell-tower. Inside the church is a statue of St. Gerard and one of the Risen Christ.

To Help You Plan Your Pilgrimage

Schedule: The shrine is open all year. The Feast of St. Gerard is celebrated on October 16 and there is a preparatory novena from October 7 to 15. On the feast day there is a Mass, distribution of the blessed Bread of St. Gerard and a Blessing of the Sick. On the 16th of every month many individuals come to the shrine to pray. Masses are celebrated at the church on Tuesdays at 3:30 p.m and Saturdays at 7:00 p.m. and can be arranged in advance for large pilgrimage groups.

For your convenience: There are washrooms, parking and a religious articles stand at the shrine. There is a ramp for the handicapped.

For further information: St. Gérard Shrine, 191, rue Principale, Weedon, Secteur Saint-Gérard, QC J0B 3J0. ☎ (819) 877-2691 or (819) 877-2395.

Also of interest: The shrine at Scotstown is to the south. (See separate entry.)

SAINT-GERMAIN-DE-KAMOURASKA

Calvary

Saint-Germain is southwest of Rivière-du-Loup on Highway 132. The Calvary has a shelter over it. It was erected in 1850 and it is attributed to Louis-Thomas Berlinguet. Nearby St. Denis has one just as old.

SAINT-JEAN-PORT-JOLI

Calvary and Lourdes Grotto

Saint-Jean-Port-Joli is on the south shore of the St. Lawrence, northeast of Quebec City and midway between Montmagny and La Pocatière on Highway 132.

This is the centre for the Quebec woodcarvers. There are about 50 woodcarvers' studios and many of them are open to the public. The parish church with its high pitched roofs and two steeples was built in 1779. It has many woodcarvings from the 18th to the 20th centuries.

At the entrance to the nearby cemetery is a Grotto to Our Lady of Lourdes. On the side of the cemetery nearest to the riverbank is a fine Calvary carved by Médard Bourgault.

A few blocks east of the parish church along the main street is an excellent example of a processional chapel. Over the entrance are folk art faces of angels.

SAINT-LÉON-DE-STANDON

Calvary

Saint-Léon is in Beauce County, on Highway 277, south of Quebec City and not far from Lac Etchemin. The Calvary was created by folk artist Pierre Bisson in 1965.

SAINT-MICHEL-DE-BELLECHASSE

Chapel of Notre-Dame-de-Lourdes

Saint-Michel is on the south shore of the St. Lawrence, about 15 kilometres northeast of Lévis on Highway 132.

This is a small local pilgrimage. The shrine was founded by Father Napoléon Laliberté in 1879, six years after he had made a pilgrimage to Lourdes, France. The chapel is perched on a point of land overlooking the river. There is also a Grotto of Our Lady of Lourdes.

The chapel is open from the first Saturday of May to the last Saturday of September. Pilgrimage day is the Sunday following August 15, the Feast of the Assumption.

SAINT-THOMAS

Shrine of Our Lady of Peace

The village of Saint-Thomas is just east of Joliette (Highway 158) on the north shore of the St. Lawrence River. It has a shrine Chapel of Our Lady of Peace established in 1931, a Grotto of Our Lady of Lourdes and a Way of the Cross. There is a diocesan pilgrimage on the Feast of the Assumption (August 15).

For further information: Saint-Thomas Parish, 830, rue Principale, P.O. Box 69, Saint-Thomas, QC J0K 3L0. ☎ and 🖷 (450) 753-3366.

SAINTE-ANNE-DE-BEAUPRÉ

Shrine of Ste. Anne de Beaupré

Ste. Anne de Beaupré is the oldest shrine in Canada, dating back to 17th-century New France, and the largest shrine to this saint in the world. Situated on the north shore of the St. Lawrence River, opposite Ile d'Orléans and 35 kilometres east of Quebec City, it is famous internationally and receives about a million and a half visitors every year.

History

In 1658 French settler Étienne Lessard offered land for a wooden chapel dedicated to Ste. Anne, the grandmother of Christ and a favourite saint of many of the settlers from Brittany. Four years later a group of sailors were shipwrecked within sight of the new church and they attributed their survival to prayers to Ste. Anne.

From this time on, stories of cures spread and pilgrims began to arrive. In 1665 Marie de l'Incarnation, living in the Ursuline Convent in Quebec City, wrote about the cures. In 1670 Bishop Laval donated the first relic of Ste. Anne, one that he had received from the Chapter of Carcassone in France.

In 1671 the Hurons came on pilgrimage from Côte Saint-Michel, establishing a tradition of Indian devotion to Ste. Anne that later spread to all regions of Canada.

In the late 17th century a new stone church was built. In the late 18th century General Wolfe's soldiers burned the village of Beaupré but left the church untouched. Nevertheless,

British control over French Canada brought a decline in the pilgrimage for several generations.

But in the middle of the 19th century there was a great revival of pilgrimage, partly due to Lourdes and La Salette in France, but also due to the arrival of the first steamships and the opening of the Grand Trunk Railway. In 1876 a larger church was opened to handle the crowds and in 1887 this church was raised to the rank of basilica by Pope Leo XIII.

In 1878 the Redemptorist Order took charge of the shrine. In 1922 the basilica was so badly ravaged by fire that a new structure had to be planned. Construction and decoration continued decade after decade as money became available until, in 1976, it was considered complete enough to be consecrated by Cardinal Roy. Today the work of embellishment continues.

The Shrine

The basilica is in the Romanesque style. It is made of granite quarried at Saint-Sebastien de Beauce and is one of the largest and most elaborate churches in North America. Rising to a height of 27 metres in the nave, it is almost 100 metres long (not including the sacristy) and 67 metres wide at the transept. At the front of the basilica is a platform with several staircases and ramps especially built for pilgrims and giving access to the main doorways to the upper church and the crypt.

The facade includes two towers with steeples rising over 100 metres, with a gilded statue of Ste. Anne standing on the gable between the towers. Beneath this, under a huge Romanesque arch, is a rose window signifying the love of God. Over the central doorway is a sculptured tympanum and frieze showing the enthroned Ste. Anne welcoming lines of pilgrims.

The nave of the church is flanked by four aisles and by huge stone columns with sculpted capitals by Emile Brunet and Maurice Lord. Around the walls are 210 stained glass windows in a splintered glass technique. The sanctuary is outstanding with an altar enclosed by a magnificent bronze tent-like structure. This ciborium symbolizes the pilgrim's encounter with God. Behind the sanctuary runs a wide semi-circular ambulatory giving access to a series of elaborate radiating chapels, each one entirely different from the others in decoration.

The famous miraculous statue of Ste. Anne carrying the child Mary stands in front of a sunburst on top of a pillar in the north transept. A short distance behind the pillar is the chapel containing the major relic given by Pope John XXIII in 1960.

The shrine has a carillon and two pipe organs. Among the chapels in the crypt is one for Eastern Rites and the tomb of Venerable Alfred Pampalon.

The Grounds

The plaza in front of the basilica is the place in which the processions form. It has a fountain. Across Royale Avenue at the foot of the hill is the Memorial Chapel made from stones of the 17th-century church. In front of the building is a pillar with a statue of Ste. Anne and a spring of water that comes from the hillside.

The next building along the avenue is the Chapel of the Holy Stairs, a three-storey Baroque structure with a replica of the Holy Stairs from Pilate's palace. Here the pilgrim climbs 28 steps on the knees, praying and meditating on the passion of Christ. You may see bouquets on the altar; the local custom is for a bride to leave her bouquet here on her wedding day.

One set of steps up the hillside leads to the convent of the Franciscan Sisters. Their chapel is always open for Adoration of the Blessed Sacrament. They have a small handicraft shop to support their missions. Another way up the hillside is along the Way of the Cross.

The Historial is a wax museum with a series of tableaux on the life of Ste. Anne and the history of Ste. Anne de Beaupré. The museum displays many artworks and *ex-votos*, such as the chasuble sent in 1666 by Anne of Austria, Queen of France.

The Cyclorama of Jerusalem is a large circular building that contains an enormous panoramic oil painting of the City of Jerusalem and its environs in the time of Christ. Visitors use binoculars to see the details.

To Help You Plan Your Pilgrimage

Schedule: The basilica is open all year: in spring, summer and fall from 6:30 a.m. to 10:00 p.m., and in winter from 6:30 a.m. to 5:00 p.m., but the busiest months are June to September. The Feast of Ste. Anne (July 26) is celebrated with candlelight processions and Masses. There is a preparatory novena July 17 to 25. There are many special pilgrimages including ones for Native people and youth. Many dioceses organize pilgrimages. For the schedule of Masses, processions, anointings of the sick, Stations of the Cross, organ recitals, etc., write for brochures or check the web site.

For your convenience: The shrine is fully equipped, has its own hospital, pastoral counselling and youth office. There is a religious bookstore and gift shop.

For further information: Secretariat of the Basilica, Sainte-Anne-de-Beaupré, QC G0A 3C0. ☎ (418) 827-3781; 🖨 (418) 827-8227; web site www.ssadb.qc.ca. To help you keep up-to-date on shrine activities, there is a monthly magazine. Write to *Annals of Ste. Anne*, P.O. Box 1000, Sainte-Anne-de-Beaupré, QC G0A 3C0. ☎ (418) 827-4538; 🖨: (418) 827-4530.

Also of interest: Many pilgrims staying in Quebec City drive out or take a bus daily to the shrine. The drive along the north shore of the St. Lawrence on the upper highway is one of the most delightful in the entire country. Along the way one can stop at Montmorency Falls or Ile d'Orléans.

SAINTE-ANNE-DE-LA-ROCHELLE

Shrine of Ste-Anne-de-la-Rochelle

The village of Sainte-Anne-de-la-Rochelle is 45 kilometres west of Sherbrooke on Highway 220.

The Parish of Ste. Anne was founded in 1857 on a small mountain that the first settlers called Rochelle, or small rock. The pilgrimage began around 1905 and liturgies were held in the parish church. In 1945 Father Albert Bruneau initiated the building of the outdoor shrine to Ste. Anne.

The Shrine

The shrine on the hill is reached by a long flight of stairs that is sometimes used as a *Scala Sancta*. There is a chapel here with a large open area in front of it surrounded by trees. There is a statue of Ste. Anne here as well as in the church. On the grounds there is a Grotto of Our Lady of Lourdes and a Grotto of the Holy Family. Around the side of the hill is a Way of the Seven Sorrows with a tomb of Ste. Anne. There is also a large cross that is illuminated at night.

To Help You Plan Your Pilgrimage

Schedule: The shrine is open in the summer months. The big pilgrimage day is the Feast of Ste. Anne (July 26), with a preparatory novena and a triduum. On the Feast of Ste. Anne there are several Masses, the veneration of the relic and a Blessing of the Sick. The Bishop of Sherbrooke celebrates the final Mass and the celebration closes with a candlelight procession.

For your convenience: There is plenty of parking on the grounds, and there are washrooms. Bring a lawn chair.

Also of interest: The whole region south of Sainte-Anne-de-la-Rochelle is a vacation area. The Abbey of Saint-Benoît-du-Lac is not far away. (See separate entry.)

SAINTE-ANNE-DES-MONTS

Shrine of Ste. Anne

Sainte-Anne-des-Monts is on the north shore of the Gaspé Peninsula by the St. Lawrence River. It is about 85 kilometres northeast of Matane by Highway 132.

Although the first parish was established here in 1815, the first chapel was built only in 1836 and the pilgrimage to Ste. Anne began in 1855. The present parish church, in a Romanesque style with double steeples, was built in 1939. It is of local granite and is quite majestic. It faces the St. Lawrence River and has a statue of Ste. Anne on its gable.

The interior, finished in 1956, is very ornate. On the semi-dome of the apse is a painting of Ste. Anne flanked by angels. There is a statue of Ste. Anne and a relic.

To Help You Plan Your Pilgrimage

Schedule: The annual pilgrimage on July 26, the Feast of Ste. Anne, draws pilgrims from all over the Gaspé Peninsula.

For your convenience: There are several hotels in the town.

For further information: Sainte-Anne-des-Monts Shrine, 5 First Avenue East, P.O. Box 578, Sainte-Anne-des-Monts, QC G0E 2G0.

Also of interest: Just 10 kilometres to the east is Tourelle, with a Grotto of Our Lady of Fatima. (See separate entry.)

SAINTE-MARIE-DE-BEAUCE

Chapel of Ste. Anne de Beauce

The village of Sainte-Marie, in the county of Beauce, is situated on the Chaudière River about 45 kilometres south of Quebec City. Take Highway 73.

The Shrine

The Chapel of Ste. Anne is a regional shrine. The original chapel was built in 1778 by the parishioners of Ste. Marie de Beauce because of their devotion to Ste. Anne and in thanksgiving after they were spared property damage from floods. It was rebuilt in stone in 1828 and 1891.

Over the entrance is a large statue of Ste. Anne carved by Henri Angers in 1928. In front is the tiny miraculous statue of Ste. Anne carved by Pierre-Noël Levasseur. There is also a painting of Ste. Anne done in 1843 by Antoine Plamondon.

To Help You Plan Your Pilgrimage

Schedule: Pilgrimage season is June to October. The big day is the Feast of Ste. Anne (July 26) when pilgrims come from all the parishes of the region. During the novena to Ste. Anne, which runs from July 17 to 26, the chapel is open from 8:00 a.m. to 9:00 p.m.

For your convenience: Food and lodging can be found in the village.

For further information: Sainte-Marie-de-Beauce Parish, 62 Notre Dame Street South, P.O. Box 1058, Sainte-Marie-de-Beauce, QC G6E 3C2. ☎ (418) 387-5467; 🖳 (418) 387-7545.

Also of interest: The Church of Ste. Marie, designed by Charles Baillairgé, is full of works of art. In the cemetery is a brick Gothic chapel dedicated to the Sacred Heart of Jesus. Built in 1879, it has a slender spire and a rose window. There are three surviving processional chapels that were built and maintained by local families. The Turcotte Chapel, also dedicated to the Sacred Heart, was built in 1924. During May people gather here for the Rosary. The Hébert Chapel, dedicated to Our Lady of Protection, was built in 1936. About 8 kilometres along the left bank of the river from the church is the Cliche Chapel, dedicated in 1885 to Our Lady of Protection. It is open all summer and there is a small gathering here for the Feast of the Assumption (August 15).

SAINTE-THÉRÈSE

Chapel of Notre-Dame-du-Perpétuel-Secours (Our Lady of Perpetual Help)

Sainte-Thérèse is north of Montreal by Highway 117 on Highway 15. The chapel is in the Monastery of the Redemptoristine Nuns, 115 west, côte Saint-Louis.

There are regular devotions to Our Lady of Perpetual Help but no pilgrimage day.

Nearby Saint-Jerome has an impressive cathedral as well. Not far away is the shrine at Lachute and the Calvary at Oka. (See separate entries.)

SCOTSTOWN

Shrine of Notre-Dame-des-Victoires

The village of Scotstown is in Compton County, about two thirds of the way from Sherbrooke to Lake Megantic. The shrine is on Highway 214 about 1 kilometre from Scotstown toward Milan.

In 1932 Moïse Lambert, who had made a promise to Mary, bought a piece of woodland by a lake and began cutting down trees to make a place for the shrine. On the highest part of the property a chalet was built on a platform. Inside is the shrine. There is also a statue of Our Lady of the Assumption facing the lake. On the grounds is an illuminated cross and an old windmill. There is an outdoor altar of polished stone for Mass for pilgrim groups and a Way of the Cross.

To Help You Plan Your Pilgrimage

Schedule: The shrine is open from May to October. The Feast of the Assumption (August 15) is the local pilgrimage day. On the evening of the feast day there is a Mass and a candlelight procession, as well as one on Sunday in May and October.

For your convenience: There are picnic tables on the grounds and a hotel in the village.

For further information: St-Paul Parish, 53 Ditton, P.O. Box 60, Scotstown, QC J0B 3B0.

SHERBROOKE

Mother Léonie Centre

Sherbrooke is in the Eastern Townships, about 170 kilometres east of Montreal. Take Highway 10 south from Montreal, or Highway 55 south from Trois-Rivières and Quebec City.

Mother Léonie

Mother Léonie was born in 1840 at L'Acadie, south of Montreal. Despite frail health she entered the Convent of the Marianites of the Holy Cross at the age of 14 and was professed at the age of 17. For eight years she taught school and cared for orphans and poor children in New York City. In 1874 she was called by the Holy Cross Fathers to Memramcook, New Brunswick, to train Acadian girls at St. Joseph's College. In 1880 she founded the Little Sisters of the Holy Family and fifteen years later moved the Motherhouse to Sherbrooke.

The aim of her order is to help with the formation of priests by doing domestic tasks in seminaries and other houses of formation and by modelling the Christian life. Before she died in 1912, her sisters were active in more than 40 locations. In 1984 she was beatified by Pope John Paul II on his visit to Canada.

The Shrine

The Mother Léonie Centre is behind the Motherhouse of the Little Sisters of the Holy Family at 1820 Galt Street West. It was built in 1968 to advance the cause of Mother Léonie among the faithful. Inside are reconstructions of the bedroom and office she used in her last years with the original furnishings. There are displays of objects relating to her life and her order. There is a small chapel here and an oratory with the tomb of Mother Léonie. Note the monument to her sculpted by Camille Racicot and placed in front of the Motherhouse.

To Help You Plan Your Pilgrimage

Schedule: The centre is open all summer daily from 10:00 to 11:00 a.m. and from 3:00 to 5:00 p.m. Groups of 30 or more should make reservations. Occasionally groups accompanied by a priest may celebrate Mass in the little chapel of the tomb or in the larger chapel in the Motherhouse.

For your convenience: The cafeteria of the University of Sherbrooke is not far from the centre.

For further information: Marie-Léonie Paradis Centre, 1820 Galt Street West, Sherbrooke, QC J1K 1H9. ☎ (819) 346-2134; 🖷 (819) 562-2578; e-mail: cmlp@globetrotter.net. The centre produces a quarterly, *Bulletin de Mère Marie Léonie.*

Also of interest: The Cathedral of St. Michael is interesting. Not far away are the shrines at Beauvoir, Notre-Dame-des-Bois, Scotstown, St-Gerard, Warwick and the Abbey of St-Benoît-du-Lac. (See separate entries.)

Shrine of Notre-Dame-du-Perpétuel-Secours (Our Lady of Perpetual Help)

The address of the church is 905 Ontario Street.

The shrine is in the Church of Notre-Dame-du-Perpétuel-Secours, founded in 1913 by the Redemptorist Fathers who had established their monastery near here in 1911. The shrine was founded in 1931 and the new church was built in 1947. In that year a painted copy of the famous icon of Our Lady of Perpetual Help, in the Church of St. Alphonsus in Rome, was bought and installed.

To Help You Plan Your Pilgrimage

Schedule: There is a pilgrimage on the third Sunday of June celebrating the Feast of Our Lady of Perpetual Help. There is Mass and a procession.

For further information: Notre-Dame-du-Perpétuel-Secours, 1331 Desgagné, Sherbrooke, QC J1J 1H5.

TOURELLE

Grotto of Our Lady of Fatima

Tourelle is 10 kilometres east of Ste-Anne-des-Monts on the north shore of the Gaspé Peninsula near the St. Lawrence River. Take Highway 132. The Grotto to Our Lady of Fatima is in front of the Church of St. Joachim. There is a Calvary in the cemetery on the hillside behind the church.

Fifty kilometres to the east along Highway 132 is Mont-Saint-Pierre with a large metal cross at the summit.

TROIS-RIVIÈRES

Tomb and Museum of Father Frédéric

The tomb and museum are at St. Maurice Street and Laviolette Street, near the St. Maurice River.

Father Frédéric

Frédéric Janssoone was born in 1838 in French Flanders. He was ordained a Franciscan in 1870 and in 1876 he asked to be transferred to the Holy Land. There he spent several years as custodian of the holy places. While on leave of absence in 1881, he was invited to visit Canada and first saw Cap-de-la-Madeleine. In his short stay he came to realize that his life was here.

It was not before 1888 that he was able to return to Cap-de-la-Madeleine. Within a matter of days he witnessed, with two others, the miracle of Our Lady of the Cape and it changed his life permanently. He became director of pilgrimages at the shrine and brought all his Holy Land experience to the project. Among other things he set up a Way of the Cross at the Cap, as well as at St-Élie de Caxton and at Pointe-aux-Trembles. At the same time he wrote and published a continuous stream of books and pamphlets. All the while he became well known for his holiness, for his preaching and for helping the poor. He died in 1916. On September 15, 1988, four years after Pope John Paul II visited Cap-de-la-Madeleine, Frédéric was beatified in Rome.

The Shrine

The shrine was founded in 1938 to promote the cause of Father Frédéric toward sainthood. The tomb is in the red brick Chapel of St. Anthony. The museum next door, at 890 St-Maurice, chronicles the life of Frédéric.

To Help You Plan Your Pilgrimage

Schedule: The shrine and museum are open every afternoon from April 1 to December 31. From June to September they are also open in the morning. August 5 is the day of Blessed Frédéric and is preceded by a triduum. On August 5 there are solemn Masses morning and evening. On the second Thursday and third Sunday of every month is a Mass in honour of Frédéric.

For further information: Frédéric-Janssoone Museum, 890 St-Maurice Street, Trois-Rivières, QC G9A 1R9. ☎ (819) 378-4864; 🖬 (819) 376-1533.

Also of interest: The cathedral has 31 stained glass windows by Nincheri. In the Monastery of the Ursuline Nuns is the Museum of the Ursulines with a great deal of religious art. The Church of St. Philip has paintings by Légaré and Frère Luc. Father Frédéric's Calvary is still at St-Élie. (See separate entry.)

VARENNES

Shrine of Ste. Anne de Varennes

Varennes is on the south shore of the St. Lawrence River opposite the east end of the Island of Montreal. Take Highway 132 east from Longueuil.

Though the parish was founded as far back as 1692, the pilgrimage did not formally begin until 1868 with the blessing of a new chapel. The large domed Church of Ste. Anne, replete with art, has recently been designated a basilica. The Chapel of Ste. Anne is a little distance from the church. Designed by architect Victor Bourgeau in the Gothic style, it has a slender spire, a trefoil-shaped window on the facade, and a statue of

Ste. Anne over the entrance. Inside is a miraculous painting of Ste. Anne dating from 1842. It was crowned by Bishop Bourget of Montreal.

To Help You Plan Your Pilgrimage

Schedule: Pilgrimage day is the Feast of Ste. Anne (July 26) and is celebrated with a Mass and a procession.

For further information: Ste. Anne Parish, 30 de la Fabrique, Varennes, QC J3X 1R1. ☎ (450) 652-2441; 🖹 (450) 652-7388; e-mail: ste-anne@enter-net.com; web site: http://www.enter-net.com/ste-anne.

Also of interest: At the other end of the village is the tiny processional Chapel to St. Joachim, the husband of Ste. Anne. Built in 1831–32, it is a pendant to the chapel of Ste. Anne. The Shrine of St. Marguerite d'Youville is also in Varennes. (See next entry.) Varennes also has a Calvary erected in 1776 by Michel Brisset.

Shrine of St. Marguerite d'Youville

The Shrine to St. Marguerite was built in 1961 of fieldstone, wood and glass. The unusual stone tower of the shrine has a large bas-relief sculpture of Mother d'Youville on it. Inside are an altar and several paintings and stained glass windows on the life of St. Marguerite. Across the street by the St. Lawrence River is a statue of her.

To Help You Plan Your Pilgrimage

Schedule: The shrine is open from 1:30 p.m. to 4:30 p.m. from Wednesday to Sunday, May 1 to October 31. Every Wednesday evening there is Mass and the Rosary. Occasionally there are other Masses, Benedictions and processions.

For your convenience: There is parking at the shrine. There are washrooms, an information office and a religious articles shop. There are accommodations and restaurants in Varennes and Montreal.

For further information: Marguerite d'Youville Shrine, 201 Sainte-Anne Street, Varennes, QC J3X 1R6. ☎ (450) 652-2873.

Also of interest: The Shrine of Ste. Anne de Varennes is nearby. (See previous entry.)

VILLE-MARIE

Grotto of Notre-Dame-de-Lourdes

Ville-Marie is on Lake Témiscamingue in northwest Quebec on the Ontario border. From North Bay take Highway 63 to Temiscaming and then 101 north.

History

In May 1886, Oblate Father P.C. Mourier and a group of settlers chose the name Ville-Marie for their settlement in honour of Mary. In 1887 the first Church of Our Lady of the Rosary was built. In 1904, the 50th anniversary of the proclamation of the Dogma of the Immaculate Conception, the Grotto of Notre-Dame-de-Lourdes was constructed by parishioners on a hilltop at the other end of the village from the church. In 1934 the pilgrimage was made diocesan.

The Shrine

Today the grotto is part of a rocky outcrop on the hilltop. There is an altar in the cave for group liturgies. There is also a Way of the Cross surrounding the grotto.

To Help You Plan Your Pilgrimage

Schedule: The shrine is open from June 24 to the end of August. The big pilgrimage day is the Feast of the Assumption, which is celebrated on the Sunday preceding August 15. Several groups come on pilgrimage at other times of the year. From the grounds there is a marvellous view of the town and of Lake Témiscamingue.

For your convenience: There are motels and restaurants in Ville-Marie.

For further information: Notre-Dame du Rosaire Shrine, P.O. Box 189, Ville-Marie, QC J0Z 3W0. ☎ (819) 629-2838; 🖷 (819) 629-3487.

Also of interest: Ville-Marie has an historic pioneer house, a summer theatre and an international regatta. At Duhamel-Ouest, a few kilometres away, is a large cross near old Fort Témiscamingue to commemorate the first chapel in the region, built by Father Laverlochère.

WARWICK

Shrine of Our Lady of Fatima

The town of Warwick is southeast of Trois-Rivières in the region known as Bois-Francs. From Highway 20 take either Highway 955/122 or Highway 162 to Victoriaville, then Highway 116 south, which runs close to Warwick.

The Shrine of Our Lady of Fatima was the idea of Sister Marie-de-la-Réparation, Superior of the Convent of the Sisters of the Assumption in the 1940s. The site, which has a beautiful panoramic view of the area, was donated by Armand Baril in 1945 and the shrine was begun in 1948. The statues of the Madonna and peasant children are in a garden setting behind the convent at 95 Saint-Louis Street.

To Help You Plan Your Pilgrimage

Schedule: The shrine is open from May 1 to October 15. The pilgrimage is largely local. There are Marian devotions during the month of May and a celebration for the Feast of the Assumption in the middle of August.

For further information: Shrine of Our Lady of Fatima, St-Médard of Warwick Parish, Warwick, QC J0L 3V0. ☎ (819) 358-2221; 🖳 (819) 358-5459.

Also of interest: The Church of St. Christophe at Arthabaska has frescoes by Suzor-Coté.

YAMASKA

Calvary

Yamaska is on the south side of the St. Lawrence River halfway between Montreal and Trois-Rivières. From Montreal take Highway 30 to Sorel and then Highway 132 to Yamaska.

The Calvary is on the main street of the village not far from the parish church. It is an *ex-voto* erected after the 1837 Rebellion by men who had been condemned to death for their part in the crisis but who were subsequently pardoned.

Also of interest: If you are driving from Trois-Rivières (Highway 55 south, then Highway 132 west), be sure to stop off at Nicolet.

The Cathedral of Nicolet is in the modern style, with plenty of curves and walls of stained glass made by Max Ingrand of France. Nicolet has other religious buildings and a new Museum of Religions.

Ontario

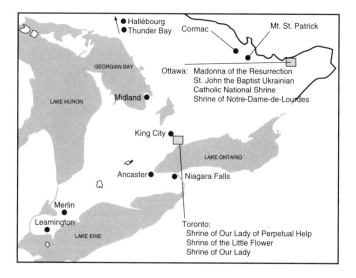

Hallébourg
Thunder Bay
Cormac
Mt. St. Patrick

GEORGIAN BAY

Ottawa: Madonna of the Resurrection
St. John the Baptist Ukrainian
Catholic National Shrine
Shrine of Notre-Dame-de-Lourdes

LAKE HURON

Midland

King City

LAKE ONTARIO

Ancaster
Niagara Falls

Merlin

Leamington

LAKE ERIE

Toronto:
Shrine of Our Lady of Perpetual Help
Shrine of the Little Flower
Shrine of Our Lady

ANCASTER

Mount Mary Immaculate Shrine

Ancaster is on the western edge of Hamilton on Highway 2. The shrine is at Mount Mary Immaculate Retreat Centre.

In 1957 the Sister Servants of Mary Immaculate instituted the annual pilgrimage in order to keep alive the Ukrainian tradition of pilgrimage that had been outlawed by the Communist government in Ukraine.

The Shrine

In the retreat centre is the shrine chapel with the icon of the Mother of Perpetual Help. On the grounds are a *Pietà* chapel, a Way of the Cross and a shrine to Our Lady of Perpetual Help with a Byzantine-style dome over it.

To Help You Plan Your Pilgrimage

Schedule: The shrine is open all year; phone ahead if you plan to go. The annual Marian pilgrimage is on the third or fourth Saturday and Sunday of June. All liturgies are in the Byzantine Rite and usually in Ukrainian. On Saturday evening there is a vigil service (in English) on themes of healing and reconciliation. On Sunday there is a sung Divine Liturgy outdoors, Solemn Blessing of the Water, Requiem service at the Sisters' cemetery, Marian devotions, Benediction and Eucharistic blessing, anointing for healing and the Sacrament of Reconciliation. All of these celebrations are in Ukrainian (the healing service may be in English). There is a special afternoon children's program conducted in English and a children's service in Ukrainian.

For your convenience: During the pilgrimage, food, books and religious articles may be purchased on the grounds. There are accommodations for about 100 pilgrims at the centre. Book in advance. Accommodations can also be found in Ancaster and in nearby Hamilton. Outside of the annual pilgrimage, private pilgrimages can be arranged if you call ahead.

For further information: Mount Mary Immaculate Retreat Centre, 437 Wilson Street East, Ancaster, ON L9G 3K4. ☎ (905) 648-4485; ▤ (905) 648-7905; e-mail: ange73@hotmail.com.

Also of interest: The Cathedral of Christ the King in Hamilton is worth visiting. Guelph has the surprising Gothic Church of Our Lady modelled after the Cathedral of Cologne, Germany.

CORMAC

Shrine of St. Ann

Cormac is in Renfrew County in the region of the upper Ottawa River. It is about 15 kilometres west of Eganville by Highway 512.

History

In 1891 the Irish community of Cormac built its first church and named the community after its first resident priest, Father James McCormac. In 1919 St. Ann's Church burned and was rebuilt in a more elaborate style.

In the 1930s the novice Bishop Nelligan of Pembroke found that the people of the diocese had a great devotion to St. Ann and so sought a place for local pilgrimage. He chose Cormac because of its location in the middle of the diocese and the pilgrimage began in 1938.

The Shrine

The shrine consists of a large fieldstone Grotto of St. Ann with a terrace in front. In the grotto is a statue of St. Ann and on the terrace is an altar for Mass.

To Help You Plan Your Pilgrimage

Schedule: The annual pilgrimage takes place on the last weekend of July. There is a preparatory triduum with a candlelight procession. The Feast of St. Ann (July 26) is observed on Sunday with a morning Mass, an afternoon healing Mass, Rosary, Benediction and application of the relic of St. Ann.

For your convenience: There are facilities for the handicapped. On Sunday food and refreshments are available on the grounds. Accommodations can be found at Eganville, Pembroke, Killaloe and Barry's Bay.

For further information: St. Ann's Parish, General Delivery, Cormac, ON K0J 1M0.

Also of interest: Nearby in Wilno is the first Canadian Polish settlement and church. The Cathedral of St. Columbkille in Pembroke is worth a visit.

HALLÉBOURG

Shrine of Ste. Anne-de-Hallébourg

Hallébourg is just east of Hearst in the north-central region of the province below James Bay. From North Bay take Highway 11.

The shrine is at the Church of Ste. Anne. Pilgrimage day is the Feast of Ste. Anne (July 26), when most of the 6,000 pilgrims who come here arrive. This diocesan pilgrimage includes a Mass and procession, and it is preceded by a triduum.

KING CITY

Shrine of Our Lady of Grace

The shrine is on the estate of Marylake in King City, just north of Toronto. From Toronto take Keele Street north. The gateway is right on Keele Street, opposite the western end of Bloomington Road.

History

The stone gateway and gatehouse may remind you of the entrance to an English country estate. Sir Henry Pellat – royalist, financier, builder of Toronto's Casa Loma and a lover of everything English – once owned this property. His estate included a dairy farm, a hunting lodge, a forest stocked with deer and elk, and an icehouse stocked with ice blocks cut from the frozen lake in winter. The estate was sold in 1936 to a Catholic group for an agricultural school and the name was changed from Lake Marie to Marylake.

In the early 1940s Cardinal McGuigan was looking for a pilgrimage place and spiritual centre for the Archdiocese of Toronto. Arrangements were made for the Augustinian Order to purchase the estate and in 1942 the Augustinians moved into the old hunting lodge, which now became Marylake – Our Lady of Grace. The title Our Lady of Grace comes from an Augustinian shrine in Lisbon, Portugal.

In 1964 Cardinal McGuigan laid the cornerstone for the new shrine building; it was dedicated in 1978 by Cardinal Carter.

The Shrine

The shrine was built by architect Stuart Cauley of local fieldstone, concrete and brick. Both the shrine and the Blessed Sacrament Chapel on the east side have a floor plan in the shape of an ellipse.

The cone-shaped bell-tower holds a 2,500-pound bell and a cross. The stained glass of the tower floods the sanctuary with light, mostly blue. In the sanctuary is the statue of Our Lady of Grace. On the south side of the church is an elaborate sculpture entitled *Our Lady's Role in Salvation History*. Sculpted by William McElcheran, it shows the tree of life winding upwards enclosing scenes representing the scriptural development of the idea of humanity's redemption through Christ.

In the Blessed Sacrament Chapel are the marble tabernacle and lectern carved by Earl Neiman. The bronze crucifix, candleholders and sanctuary lamp are by Maria Neiman, who also made the terra-cotta Stations of the Cross in the church.

The organ is a combination of two major instruments – one from the Eaton estate and one from the Seagram estate. It has over 3,000 pipes.

The grounds include hundreds of acres of rolling hills, woods and a kettle moraine lake. There are still some buildings from the old Pellat estate but these have been transformed for new uses. Since 1965 the monastery has been the provincial headquarters of the Canadian Augustinians. There is a convent and a retreat house, which operates during the fall and winter months. Not far from the shrine is a pilgrim's chapel for private prayer and a Stations of the Cross.

To Help You Plan Your Pilgrimage

Schedule: The shrine is open all year. There is Mass every Sunday at 9:00 a.m., with Benediction/Rosary and Evening Prayer every Sunday at 5:30 p.m. Holy Hour for vocations is every Thursday from 7:30 to 8:30 p.m.

There are many organized pilgrimages from Toronto, especially Italian, Portuguese and Filipino groups. Pilgrimage groups can arrange in advance for their own Mass, procession, etc.

For your convenience: The shrine is accessible to the handicapped. There are washrooms in the shrine building and on the grounds, parking and a picnic area on the grounds. There is a religious articles shop by the shrine.

For further information: Marylake, P.O. Box 550, King City, ON L0G 1K0. ☎ (905) 833-5368; ▤ (905) 833-5569.

LEAMINGTON

Shrine of St. Anthony the Great

Leamington is southeast of Windsor on Lake Erie (Highway 3).

This shrine is run by the Maronites, an ancient Eastern rite that uses the Syriac and Arabic languages in liturgy. The Maronites are the major church in Lebanon. St. Anthony the Great, the father of Christian monasticism, lived in the Egyptian desert in the third and fourth centuries.

For further information: Shrine of St. Anthony the Great, 58-280 Talbot Street East, Leamington, ON N8H 3W2.

MERLIN

Our Lady of the Rosary Shrine

Our Lady of the Rosary shrine was relocated from St. Mary's, Ontario, to St. Patrick's Church, Merlin, in 1999. The shrine is on the 10th Line, Raleigh, Township, R.R.5, Merlin, 15 minutes from Chatham or Tilbury and 40 minutes from Windsor. The shrine features the World Pilgrim Statue of Our Lady of Fatima that for years was taken around the world by Father Patrick Moore to publicize the Fatima message of peace.

To Help You Plan Your Pilgrimage

Schedule: The shrine is open every day of the year for private prayer and meditation. There are four trails to enjoy: The Rosary

Trail, The Stations of the Cross Trail, The Saints Trail and The Approved Apparitions Trail. Yearly Shrine Days are July 2, 13 and 16 plus August 13 to 22 (10 consecutive days). Mass is at 11:00 a.m. every day with a Rosary Procession at 1:30, followed by a sermon by the Shrine Director and Benediction. *For your convenience:* There is a picnic area, lots of parking (including for buses) and washroom facilities. Visitors may wish to bring lawn chairs and their lunch; there is room for 3000 to gather.

For further information: ☎ and 🖳 (519) 689-7760; e-mail: olshrine@sympatico.ca.

MIDLAND

Canadian Martyrs' Shrine

The shrine is just east of Midland on Highway 12, overlooking the River Wye.

The Canadian Martyrs

The Shrine of the Canadian Martyrs honours 17th-century Jesuit priests and their lay helpers who worked among the Hurons and eventually died for their faith.

From their stockade at Ste. Marie, the "blackrobes" went out to preach the gospel in the Huron villages. The steady stream of Hurons coming to Ste. Marie on pilgrimage prompted Rome to give it recognition as a place of pilgrimage in 1644.

The work of Jean de Brébeuf, who had the status of a Huron chief, and of Isaac Jogues, Gabriel Lalemant, Indian convert

Joseph Chiwatenwha, and their associates, was so great that by 1648 two thirds of the Hurons had been baptized.

The Iroquois were rivals of the Hurons in the fur trade and in the late 1640s regularly invaded and plundered Huron territory. In 1648 the Iroquois destroyed the mission of St. Joseph II, killed many villagers and took the rest prisoner. One by one the blackrobes were caught and killed. Finally in 1649 Brébeuf and Lalemant were captured at the mission station of St. Ignace and died after frightful tortures.

The remaining Jesuits and their Huron friends decided to withdraw for safety to Christian Island on Georgian Bay after setting fire to Ste. Marie. Here they built Ste. Marie II and fortified it. But disease and starvation took a terrible toll. Huronia was disintegrating and within a year the Jesuits and Hurons abandoned everything and sought the safety of Quebec.

So ended a true Canadian saga. But the faith remained alive among Huron refugees and slowly it spread among other tribes. The story of Ste. Marie was kept alive in the Jesuit Relations of New France, though for the next two centuries the site was deserted. In 1844 Jesuit Father Pierre Chazelle was the first to begin investigative work on the site of Ste. Marie. In 1925, the 300th anniversary of the arrival of the Jesuits in Huronia, the Martyrs were beatified, and in 1926 the Martyrs' Shrine was built across the road from Ste. Marie.

In 1930 the Canadian Martyrs were canonized in Rome by Pope Pius XI. In 1940 the Jesuits became owners of the site once again and full archaeological work began. Finally in 1964 the Jesuits entered into an agreement with the Ontario Government and the present historical replica of Ste. Marie, the first European settlement in Ontario, was built.

The Shrine

The shrine is a large grey stone church in the Gothic style with twin towers and spires. Inside, the elaborate reliquary of the martyrs is kept on a side altar. Behind the main altar is a large painting of the eight martyrs together. Around the walls is a German-painted Stations of the Cross. In the basement is the Filion Centre with a statue of Joseph Chiwatenwha, memorabilia and art. On his Canadian visit of 1984, Pope John Paul II blessed the sick in the church and addressed a large crowd outside. It was here that he received the highest honour of the Natives of Canada – an eagle feather.

The grounds include a Grotto of Our Lady of Huronia, a bronze Way of the Cross, an Aboriginal park, the papal visit altar and monument, and the tercentenary monument. There are also Italian, Filipino, Polish, Portuguese and German shrines, and Lithuanian, Croatian, Slovene, Belarussian and Slovak crosses. There is a statue of Kateri Tekakwitha, a fountain honouring St. Joseph, a garden and pond of St. Theresa of the Child Jesus, and a lookout. Along the River Wye is a walkway to Brébeuf's grave.

**To Help You Plan
Your Pilgrimage**

Schedule: The shrine is open from the Victoria Day weekend until Thanksgiving weekend. The Feast of the Canadian Martyrs is celebrated on the Saturday closest to September 26th. A novena precedes it. There is a Polish pilgrimage on foot, a Native pilgrimage, a Spanish pilgrimage, and many other ethnic pilgrimages. Please write or check the web site for schedules of Masses, processions, veneration of the relics, Blessing of the Sick, etc.

For your convenience: The shrine is fully equipped. French, as well as English, is understood here. There are accommodations in Midland.

For further information: Canadian Martyrs' Shrine, Midland, ON L4R 4K5. ☎ (705) 526-3788; 🖷 (705) 526-1546; e-mail: shrine@jesuits.ca; web site: www.jesuits.ca/martyrs-shrine. The shrine produces a magazine, *Martyrs' Shrine Message*, that provides updates on events at the shrine.

Also of interest: The reconstructed Ste. Marie-among-the-Hurons is just across the highway. St. Ignace II, one of the 12 original mission stations and the one where Brébeuf and Lalemant died, is 10 kilometres east of the shrine. Mass is celebrated there every Wednesday afternoon in July and August. Christian Island, the site of Ste. Marie II, is now a Native reservation. It has a ferry service and camping sites. At Carhagouha, west of

Penetanguishene, there is a Mass on August 12 commemorating the first Mass in Ontario (1615). In Penetanguishene is St. Anne's Memorial Church, built in commemoration of the Jesuit martyrs and Indian believers. (See separate entry.) Much further afield but closely tied to the history of the Midland shrine is the shrine at Auriesville, State of New York, where Kateri Tekakwitha was born and where three of the martyrs died. Also related is the old Huron shrine at Loretteville just outside Quebec City and the Jesuit Chapel in Quebec City. (See separate entries.)

MOUNT ST. PATRICK

St. Patrick's Well

Mount St. Patrick is near Renfrew. From Renfrew take Highway 132 for 22 kilometres and turn left at the Mt. St. Patrick sign. Just before you get to the new cemetery by the church, turn right to the old cemetery. The holy well is at the back of the old cemetery.

Holy wells are part of the Irish tradition of devotion and pilgrimage. This is one of the few in Canada. There is a tiny shrine of Our Lady of Perpetual Help over the well. Only a few people can get into the shrine at a time.

The Church of St. Patrick has Italian frescoes.

NIAGARA FALLS

Shrine of Our Lady of Peace

The shrine sits on the Niagara escarpment overlooking the Horseshoe Falls.

Shrine of Our Lady of Peace, Niagara Falls, Ontario, Canada

History

The little stone church was built in 1837 as the parish Church of St. Edward the Confessor. Niagara Falls, Ontario, was a stopping point for the Underground Railroad, which was used to carry escaped slaves from the United States to Canada in the middle of the 19th century. In 1861, with the American Civil War in progress, Pope Pius IX changed the name of the parish church to Our Lady of Peace and designated it a place of pilgrimage, noting that the rainbows by the falls were, like the rainbow in the Book of Genesis, a sign of the covenant between God and the human race. The hope was that prayers for peace here would help bring an end to the war.

To Help You Plan Your Pilgrimage

Schedule: There are no special pilgrimage days. The church is open only during services but arrangements can be made in advance for other times. (Weekend services are Saturdays at 7:00 p.m. and Sundays at 9:30 and 11:00 a.m. Weekday services are Mondays and Wednesdays at 7:00 p.m. and Tuesdays and Thursdays at 7:30 a.m.) Inside the church is a statue of the Virgin Mary. Weekend Masses are on Saturday evening and Sunday morning.

For further information: Our Lady of Peace Parish, 7021 Stanley Avenue, Niagara Falls, ON L2G 7B7. ☎ (905) 358-3791; 🖷 (905) 358-1872; e-mail: olp@vaxxine.com; web site: www.carmelniagara.com/olp.htm.

Also of interest: On the property of the neighbouring Carmelite Monastery is a plaque telling the history of the shrine. The Carmelite chapel is well worth a visit. The Niagara Falls Art Gallery has William Kurelek's series of 160 paintings on the Passion of Christ according to St. Matthew. Near the Rainbow Bridge is a memorial plaque to Father Hennepin, one of the first Europeans to see the Falls and the first to write about it.

OTTAWA

Madonna Della Risurrezione Shrine (Madonna of the Resurrection)

The shrine is in the parish of the same name on Fisher Avenue, south of the Experimental Farm.

The Shrine

The parish was founded and a pilgrimage instituted in 1980 by Oblate Father Antonio Ostan to serve the largely Italian community south and west of the Italian parish of St. Anthony of Padua. The inside of the church is modern. In the sanctuary, in front of a round stained glass window, is a statue of the Madonna of the Resurrection.

In the basement of the church is a mosaic of the Madonna of the Resurrection by artist Alex von Swoboda. In 1984 a copy of this picture was presented to Pope John Paul II on his visit to Ottawa. When he returned to Rome the pope sent a text of a special Mass to be said on the Feast of the Madonna of the Resurrection.

To Help You Plan Your Pilgrimage

Schedule: Pilgrimage time is the last weekend in May. There is a little fair with food, dancing and games in a nearby recreation centre. The celebration peaks on Sunday morning with an Italian Mass on the front steps of the church. The streets are blocked off and there is a procession through the neighbourhood. The Feast of the Assumption (August 15) is celebrated with an outdoor Mass.

For further information: Madonna della Risurrezione Parish, 1621 Fisher Avenue, Ottawa, ON K2C 1X8. ☎ (613) 723-4657; 🖳 (613) 723-3084.

Also of interest: The Ukrainian National Shrine is just to the east. (See next entry.)

St. John the Baptist Ukrainian Catholic National Shrine

One of the newest Canadian shrines, it is located on a superb site bounded by Heron Road and the Rideau Canal.

History

Ukrainian Catholics first came to Canada in 1891, fleeing persecution in Czarist Russia. Most of them settled on the Canadian prairies. The Ukrainians in Ottawa first formed a parish in 1914 and called it St. John the Baptist.

By the late 1970s parishioners were making plans for their fourth church building. At the 1980 Ukrainian Catholic National Congress in Edmonton, the idea developed that the new Ottawa church could be built as a national shrine to celebrate the 1988 Millennium of Christianity in Ukraine.

In 1984 the cornerstone was blessed by Pope John Paul II and was laid the next year. The first liturgy was celebrated at Easter 1987, and the next month Bishop Isadore Borecky officially opened and blessed the church.

The Novalis Guide to Canadian Shrines

The Shrine

The Ukrainian Catholic National Shrine was designed by Julian Jastremsky in the Byzantine style, with onion-shaped domes. The nave of the church with its barrel vaults and central dome is remarkably light and airy. The dome sits on pendentives and the ribs of the dome form a white star.

In the centre aisle, just in front of the pews, is the table-like tetrapod used during blessings, baptisms, marriages and funerals. On the altar is a tabernacle shaped like a church with five domes and icon-covered sides.

In 1991, the centennial of the first emigration of Ukrainians to Canada, a new chapel was dedicated with an icon of the Mother of Perpetual Help, an image traditionally given prominence in every home in Western Ukraine.

To Help You Plan Your Pilgrimage

Schedule: The shrine is open all year; visits may be arranged by appointment. The annual pilgrimage is the first Sunday in October. Divine Liturgy is celebrated on Sunday morning. Pilgrimage groups can arrange for the liturgy in advance. For special occasions a public prayer liturgy called a *Moleben* is celebrated.

For your convenience: English as well as Ukrainian is spoken, and many Orthodox and Catholics of the Roman rite come here. Parking is available. There are washrooms on the lower level of the shrine. On Sunday, religious articles and Ukrainian crafts, such as decorated Easter eggs and embroideries, are sold.

For further information: Director, St. John the Baptist Ukrainian Catholic National Shrine, 952 Green Valley Crescent, Ottawa, ON K2C 3K7. ☎ (613) 723-1673. ▤ (613) 723-9879; e-mail: pastor@st-john-baptist-shrine.ca.

Also of interest: Holy Spirit Ukrainian Catholic Seminary is a few blocks west of the shrine at 1030 Baseline Road. Metropolitan Sheptytsky Institute of Eastern Christian Studies is at 249 Main Street. Assumption of the Blessed Virgin Ukrainian Orthodox Cathedral is at 1000 Byron Avenue, and the Ukrainian Community Centre is at 911-A Carling Avenue.

Shrine of Notre-Dame-de-Lourdes

The shrine is at Cantin and Montfort, one block over from the church of the same name.

History

This diocesan shrine was established in 1871 by French-born Cyprian Triolle in Cyrville, and moved to Eastview (now Vanier) in 1887. In 1947 the shrine prepared for the Marian Congress by hosting the statue of Notre-Dame-du-Cap (Our Lady of the Cape), which was then touring the country.

The Shrine

Notre-Dame-de-Lourdes Church is a modern structure in white stucco with a distinctive blue peak on its roof. To the side of the church is an unusual bell-tower dedicated on the 100th anniversary of the parish in 1987.

The shrine is surrounded on three sides by condominiums and apartment buildings. Around it run the 14 Stations of the Cross, each a moulded and painted plaque set in a wooden house-like structure with a cross on top. The highest point of the land is crowned with a Calvary group with an altar in front. Lower down, at the end of the Stations, is the Lourdes Grotto with another altar. Nearby is a grouping of *ex-votos* and a statue of St. Louis de Montfort. People come here in winter and there is a hut full of vigil lights burning all winter.

To Help You Plan Your Pilgrimage

Schedule: The shrine is open all year. The Feast of the Assumption is celebrated on August 15. There is also a novena in mid-July that finishes on the Feast of Our Lady of Mount Carmel. Masses are celebrated in the grotto on Sunday mornings at 12 noon. Stations of the Cross are preached outdoors on the first Friday of the month, from June through to the end of August. The Rosary is prayed weekdays in the evening and on Sunday afternoon. A Blessing of the Sick takes place on the Feast of the Assumption.

For your convenience: There is a parking lot by the church and a smaller one by the grotto. There are washrooms in the church and in the small house by the grotto parking lot. Everything is accessible to the handicapped. Religious articles are on sale at the grotto on Sundays.

For further information: Notre-Dame-de-Lourdes Shrine, 435 Montreal Road, Vanier, ON K1K 0V2. ☎ (613) 741-4175; 🖫 (613) 741-2820.

Also of interest: Next to the grotto is Notre Dame Cemetery, with graves of prominent Canadians such as Prime Minister Wilfred Laurier, painter Jean Dallaire, and folklorist Marius Barbeau. Notre Dame Basilica on Sussex Drive, in the old market area of Ottawa, has an extremely elaborate high altar and sanctuary carved by Philippe Hébert and others. In the National Gallery across from the basilica is the restored chapel of the Rideau Street Convent.

PENETANGUISHENE

St. Anne's Memorial Jesuit Church

The Shrine
Only 12 kilometres from Canadian Martyrs Shrine in Midland (see separate entry) is St. Anne's Memorial Jesuit Church, a beautiful and historic church built to honour the eight Canadian Martyrs killed in the 17th century. Built under the direction of Fr. Theophile Laboureau of France, who arrived in Penetanguishene in 1873, the Romanesque church opened its doors in 1902.The church features murals of the Canadian Martyrs painted on the walls and ceiling; twin spires were added in 1999.

To Help You Plan Your Pilgrimage

Schedule: The church is open every day, with a daily Mass at 7:15 p.m. Sunday Masses are on Saturdays at 7:00 p.m. in English, on Sundays at 8:00 a.m. and 11:00 a.m. in French, and at 9:30 a.m. in English.

For further information: St. Anne's Parish, 28 Robert St. W., Penetanguishene, ON L9M 1N2. Phone (705) 549-2560; fax (705) 549-4746.

THUNDER BAY

Shrine of the Sacred Heart of Jesus

This tiny shrine is on Mount McKay on the Ojibwa Reservation just south of Thunder Bay. Take Highway 61B south.

The Jesuits came to this area in 1848 and set up a mission for the Indians. In 1888 Jesuit Father Joseph Hébert built a chapel on the mountain. The Shrine of the Sacred Heart of Jesus commemorates that chapel and is built with stones from the old chapel. From this height there is a beautiful view of Thunder Bay and Lake Superior.

TORONTO

Shrine of Our Lady of Perpetual Help

This is an example of a downtown shrine that has a permanent novena but no special pilgrimage day.

St. Patrick's Parish was founded in 1861 by the Irish. The present church, a large grey stone building in the Romanesque style, was built in 1912. Inside are many stained glass windows, including rose windows and a long series on the life of Christ. Today the church is in Chinatown and serves a Chinese Catholic community and a German community.

The shrine is in the left transept. It has a copy of a famous icon. In the late 19th century, Pope Pius IX gave the ancient icon of the Mother of Perpetual Help to the Redemptorist Order with the mandate to make her known throughout the world. St. Patrick's is Toronto's Redemptorist parish and the novenas began here early in the 20th century. Around 2,000 people come for the devotions every Wednesday.

**To Help You Plan
Your Pilgrimage**

Schedule: The church is open daily from 7:00 a.m. to 6:00 p.m. (Wednesdays to 8:00 p.m.) There are novenas on Wednesdays, as well as daily and Sunday Masses.

For further information: St. Patrick's Church, 141 McCaul Street, Toronto, ON M5T 1W3. ☎ (416) 598-3269; 📠 (416) 598-3869.

Also of interest: St. Paul's Catholic Church (93 Power Street at Queen Street East) is worth a visit. It is in the style of an Italian Renaissance basilica with a barrel-vaulted nave and a triple apse. Gothic-styled St. Paul's Anglican Church (Bloor at Jarvis) is the largest church in Toronto and the place where Pope John Paul II met leaders of other faith traditions in 1984.

Shrine of the Little Flower

The shrine is part of the Church of St. Theresa, a building in the Spanish style, with red-tiled roofs and a bell-tower. St. Theresa of Lisieux, the saint of the little way of spiritual perfection, was canonized in 1925. Around that time devotions to her were begun at St. Michael's Cathedral, but in 1933 they were moved to the new Parish of St. Theresa in Scarborough.

**To Help You Plan
Your Pilgrimage**

Schedule: Every Tuesday at 7:15 p.m. there is a novena to St. Theresa with exposition of the Blessed Sacrament, Mass, prayers and blessing with the relic. In late September there is a triduum leading up to the Feast of Theresa of the Child Jesus (October 1), when there is a special Mass. Pilgrimage groups are welcome.

For further information: Secretary, Shrine of the Little Flower, St. Theresa Church, 2559 Kingston Road, Scarborough, ON M1M 1M1. ☎ (416) 261-7498; 🖳 (416) 261-2901; e-mail: parish@st-theresa-shrine.org; web site: www.st-theresa-shrine.org.

Shrine to Our Lady

The shrine is in St. Michael's Cathedral, downtown at Bond and Shuter Streets, just east of Yonge Street.

The altar of Mary is on the left side of the nave at the halfway mark. The statue of the Virgin is in an elaborate wooden niche surrounded by a huge painting by Czech artist Vaclav Vaca. The painting has the symbols of Mary, for example the Mystical Rose, and four large angels each blowing a trumpet and carrying a crown. In the middle of each crown is a representation of a world-famous Marian shrine: Fatima, Lourdes, Guadalupe and Czestochowa.

There is a religious articles shop at the entrance to the cathedral.

Also of interest: St. Michael's Choir School is nearby. A block south on Bond Street is the large Metropolitan United Church, and two blocks south is historic St. James Anglican Cathedral. A block north on Bond Street is St. George Greek Orthodox Church, formerly the Holy Blossom Synagogue.

Manitoba

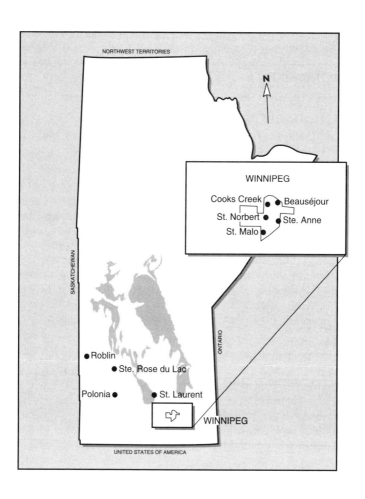

NORTHWEST TERRITORIES

N

WINNIPEG

Cooks Creek   ● Beauséjour
St. Norbert ●   ● Ste. Anne
St. Malo ●

SASKATCHEWAN

ONTARIO

● Roblin
● Ste. Rose du Lac
Polonia ●   ● St. Laurent

WINNIPEG

UNITED STATES OF AMERICA

BEAUSÉJOUR

Shrine of Notre-Dame-de-La-Salette

Beauséjour is on Highway 44, about 40 kilometres north-east of Winnipeg.

The shrine is a place of pilgrimage for the Diocese of St. Boniface. On the hill are several statues of Mary, each one of a different La Salette apparition.

There are hotels in Beauséjour and camping in Brokenhead River Park.

COOKS CREEK

Grotto of Our Lady of Lourdes

Cooks Creek is about 25 kilometres northeast of Winnipeg. Take Highways 213 and 212.

History

Cooks Creek was one of the first places in Manitoba settled by Ukrainians. By 1910 over 1,000 Ukrainians had arrived here. In that year Metropolitan Sheptytsky visited from the Ukraine and the Ukrainian Catholic Church in Canada started to take shape.

Oblate Father Philip Ruh was part of this development. An architect born in Alsace, France, he came to Canada in 1912. After arriving in the parish at Cooks Creek in 1930, he inspired the parishioners to build the magnificent Church of the Immaculate Conception, also known as the Prairie Cathedral. It was finished in 1952. Ruh was also responsible for the grotto.

The Shrine

The church is in the Byzantine style with nine cupolas and several semi-domes. The stone is decorated with geometric Ukrainian designs. Inside is an icon of the Mother of Perpetual Help. There are 92 stained glass windows. On the grounds is a free-standing domed bell-tower. The bells are the gift of Father Ruh's home parish in Alsace. The grotto is dedicated to Our Lady of Lourdes and there is also a Calvary grouping here.

To Help You Plan Your Pilgrimage

Schedule: The shrine is open on weekends from Victoria Day in May, June and September. It is open daily during July and

August from noon until 8:00 p.m. Tours are available. The annual pilgrimage is on the Feast of the Assumption (the weekend nearest to August 15). During the summer, local parishes organize their own pilgrimages here.

For your convenience: Accommodations can be found in Winnipeg.

For further information: Immaculate Conception Church, Box 35, Group 23, R.R. #2, Dugald, MN R0E 0K0. ☎ (204) 444-2478; 🖳 (204) 222-3756; e-mail: mwpage@icenter.net; web site: www.go.to/cookscreek.

Also of interest: In Winnipeg is Sts. Vladimir and Olga Ukrainian Catholic Cathedral, and the important Ukrainian Cultural and Educational Centre. The shrine at Beauséjour is just east of Cooks Creek. (See separate entry.) There is a heritage museum at St. Michael's Church in Cooks Creek.

POLONIA

Shrine of Our Lady of Czestochowa

Polonia is just south of Riding Mountain National Park in southwestern Manitoba. From Neepawa take Highway 5 north and then Highway 265 west.

The present Church of St. Elizabeth of Hungary was finished in 1902. In 1959 a painting of Our Lady of Czestochowa, the patroness of Poland, was installed over the main altar. That same year a grotto in honour of Our Lady of Lourdes was built next to the church, and the pilgrimage began.

To Help You Plan Your Pilgrimage

Schedule: The annual pilgrimage day is the third Sunday in July, celebrated with the Rosary, Reconciliation and an outdoor Mass at the grotto. The celebration alternates between English one year and Polish the next year.

For your convenience: There are accommodations in Neepawa.

For further information: St. Dominic's Church, P.O. Box 926, Neepawa, MN R0J 1H0.

Also of interest: Minnedosa to the west has a game farm.

ROBLIN

Grotto of Our Lady of Perpetual Help

Roblin is about 95 kilometres west of Dauphin, near the Saskatchewan border. This grotto is located next to the Ukrainian Catholic Church of the Transfiguration on Highway 83.

Planned by Redemptorist Father Joseph Denischuk in 1950, it contains a mosaic icon of Our Lady of Perpetual Help made in Rome.

To Help You Plan Your Pilgrimage

Schedule: The grotto is open 24 hours a day, seven days a week. The Feast of the Transfiguration is celebrated at the church on the Sunday nearest to August 6. The Byzantine Rite liturgy is in English and Ukrainian. The Feast of the Immaculate Heart of Mary (the last Sunday of May) is celebrated as Youth Day. The Feast of Our Lady of the Rosary is celebrated on the first Sunday of October.

For your convenience: There are washrooms and parking on the grounds.

For further information: Grotto of Our Lady of Perpetual Help, St. Vladimir's College, Roblin, MN R0L 1P0. ☎ (204) 937-2173; 🖳 (204) 937-8265; Ukrainian Catholic Church ☎ (204) 937-3806.

Also of interest: The Ukrainian shrine at Yorkton, Saskatchewan, is 80 kilometres to the west. (See separate entry.)

SAINTE-ANNE

Shrine of Sainte-Anne-des-Chênes

Sainte-Anne is about 30 kilometres southeast of Winnipeg. Take the Trans-Canada Highway and, just past Dufresne, turn south on Highway 12.

History

One of the most interesting phenomena of the early church in Canada was the spread of devotions from Brittany, France, to Quebec and then to other parts of Canada. In 1867 the first chapel was built at Pointe-des-Chênes and Oblate Father Joseph Lefloch from Brittany asked that it be called after Ste-Anne. That was the year of Canada's Confederation and the year that the pilgrimages began.

The most important of the early pastors of Ste-Anne-des-Chênes was Quebecer Father Louis-Raymond Giroux. When the Red River Rebellion started at Ste-Anne-des-Chênes in 1869, he was chaplain of Louis Riel's garrison at Fort Garry.

With the opening of the present larger church in 1898, the pilgrimages to Ste-Anne-des-Chênes increased, drawing many settlers who were already familiar with Ste-Anne-de-Beaupré in the east. In 1916 the Redemptorists, who ran the shrine at Beaupré, took over the Shrine of Ste-Anne-des-Chênes.

The Shrine

The present brick church is very beautiful, with a tall Gothic tower and spire. Inside is a statue similar to the one at Ste-Anne-de-Beaupré. There are four stained glass windows created by the same artist who created those at Ste-Anne-de-Beaupré, Labouret of Paris, France.

To Help You Plan Your Pilgrimage

Schedule: Pilgrimage day is on the Feast of Ste. Anne (July 26). There are devotions to Ste. Anne and a solemn Mass in the church, and a candlelight procession outside.

For your convenience: There are motels along the Trans-Canada Highway and in Winnipeg.

For further information: Redemptorist Fathers, P.O. Box 39, Sainte-Anne, MN R0A 1R0.

Also of interest: Sainte-Anne has a pioneer museum. At Winnipeg's St. Boniface stands the facade of the historic St. Boniface Cathedral. From among the ruins rises the futuristic new cathedral. In the churchyard is the grave of Louis Riel, now considered the Father of Manitoba.

ST. LAURENT

Grotto of Our Lady of Lourdes

St. Laurent is near Lake Manitoba, about 100 kilometres northwest of Winnipeg on Highway 6. The grotto is on the grounds of the Convent of the Franciscan Sisters.

The grotto was built during the Ottawa Marian Congress in 1947 by local Oblate novices.

To Help You Plan Your Pilgrimage

Schedule: The local pilgrimage day is the Feast of the Assumption (August 15).

For your convenience: There are hotels and camping in the cottage country nearby.

For further information: St. Laurent Parish, P.O. Box 132, St. Laurent, MN R0C 2S0.

Also of interest: There is a Métis cultural festival in August.

ST. MALO

Shrine of Notre-Dame-de-Lourdes

St. Malo is a French village about 55 kilometres south of Winnipeg. Take Highway 59. The shrine is by the Rat River.

By the Grotto of Our Lady of Lourdes are an altar and benches. There is a Stations of the Cross.

To Help You Plan Your Pilgrimage

Schedule: Pilgrimage day is the Feast of the Assumption (August 15).

For your convenience: There is a place for picnicking and parking. There is a hotel in the village and camping in St. Malo Provincial Recreation Park.

ST. NORBERT

Shrine of Notre-Dame-du-Bon-Secours (Our Lady of Good Help)

St. Norbert is on the southern edge of Winnipeg. Take Highway 75 to rue de l'Église (Church Street). The shrine is by the Church of St. Norbert.

This is not a shrine of pilgrimage but a wayside shrine, a fine example of the type that once existed in predominantly Catholic rural areas of Canada. This one is a wooden chapel with one side open to the outdoors. Inside is an altar and a statue of Notre-Dame-du-Bon-Secours in a niche above it. The simple coffered ceiling has painted scenes from the life of Mary.

The chapel was built in 1875 as a thanksgiving offering for a Métis victory during the Red River Resistance. The Métis, who wanted to join Confederation (in order to have the same religious and language guarantees as Quebec), were afraid that the Ontario surveyors would take away their land. They were successful in preventing the surveyors from coming north on the Pembina Trail by building a barricade across the trail and defending it.

Also of interest: Behind the parish church is the Red River with the remains of dikes from the Winnipeg flood of 1950. Not far away is Parc La Barrière, a nature reserve that commemorates the barricade on the Pembina Trail. On rue du Monastère (Monastery Road) are the ruins of the Trappist Monastery of Our Lady of the Prairies. The St. Norbert Provincial Heritage Park on Turnbull Drive interprets early French-Canadian settlement of the region.

STE. ROSE DU LAC

Grotto of Our Lady of Lourdes

If you are in the cattle country southeast of Dauphin, you might like to visit the grotto in Dollard Park on the Turtle River. Ste. Rose du Lac is about 85 kilometres north of Neepawa by Highway 5.

Further west on Highway 5 is Roblin, which also has a grotto. (See separate entry.)

Saskatchewan

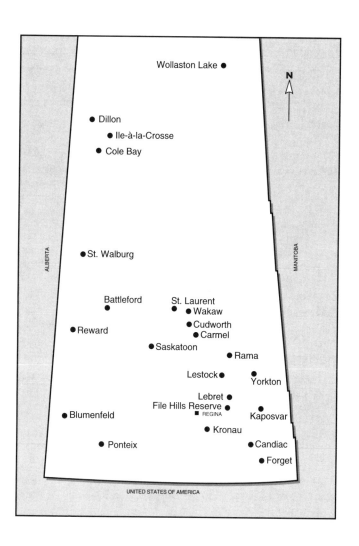

Wollaston Lake ●

N

● Dillon
● Ile-à-la-Crosse
● Cole Bay

ALBERTA

MANITOBA

● St. Walburg

Battleford
●

St. Laurent
●   ● Wakaw
● Cudworth
● Carmel

● Reward

● Saskatoon

● Rama

Lestock ●

Yorkton ●

Lebret ●
File Hills Reserve ●
■ REGINA

● Blumenfeld

Kaposvar ●

● Kronau

● Ponteix

● Candiac

● Forget

UNITED STATES OF AMERICA

BATTLEFORD

Grotto of Our Lady of Lourdes

Battleford is on the North Saskatchewan River, northwest of Saskatoon. The grotto is just south of Battleford on the Oblate farm.

The grotto was built by two Oblate brothers in 1957. After years of neglect it was restored in 1979.

There is an annual local pilgrimage on the Feast of the Assumption (August 15).

BLUMENFELD

Our Lady of Sorrows Grotto

Blumenfeld is in the region where the South Saskatchewan River flows into Alberta, about 15 kilometres south of Prelate. The area was settled in 1908 by German Catholics from Rumania. The present church of Saints Peter and Paul was built in 1915. The church is now a heritage site.

History

During the Dirty Thirties when crops were meagre and there were droughts and dust storms all across the prairies, the parish priest, Oblate Father Henry Kelz, had to move in with parishioners for two years because there was no money for the upkeep of the rectory. However, in the midst of hardship the pastor and the parishioners planned and built the shrine, carting the stones long distances to Blumenfeld. It was blessed on August 5, 1936, when the first pilgrimage took place.

The Shrine

Today the Grotto of Our Lady of Sorrows sits on a grassy terrace near the church. For pilgrimages, the doors to the shrine holding a statue of the *Pietà* are opened. There is a Calvary above it.

To Help You Plan Your Pilgrimage

Schedule: There are gatherings at the grotto during the months of June, July and August. Pilgrimage day is usually the Sunday nearest to the Feast of Saints Peter and Paul (June 29). There is a Mass and procession.

For your convenience: There are accommodations and restaurants a few miles north in Prelate and Leader.

For further information: The Ursuline Sisters, P.O. Box 220, Prelate, SK S0N 2B0.

Also of interest: St. Angela's Convent in Prelate has a small outdoor Marian shrine and a museum.

CANDIAC

Calvary Memorial Shrine

Candiac is a Polish settlement on Highway 48, southeast of Regina.

History

At the beginning of the 20th century, Polish-born Father Francis Pander was appointed pastor of the area. Pander started a newspaper, an athletic club and a musical band, and taught the Polish language and catechism. In the 1930s he organized the whole community to build the Calvary Shrine north of Candiac and later to move it to Candiac. After his death in 1957 the shrine quickly decayed. It was only in the late 1970s that interest in it revived.

The Shrine

Today the shrine is functioning again. It has a Stations of the Cross in a series of 14 miniature houses and a larger Calvary house. It also has a tower of the Virgin Mary. Made of red bricks and concrete blocks, the tower has shutters that open outward to reveal an icon of the Assumption of Mary.

To Help You Plan Your Pilgrimage

Schedule: Local pilgrimage day is the Feast of the Assumption, celebrated on the fourth Sunday of July.

For further information: Linda Clapit ☎ (306) 424-2720.

CARMEL

Our Lady of Mount Carmel

Carmel is about 90 kilometres east of Saskatoon along Highway 5, and 6 kilometres north.

History

The area was settled after 1903, mainly by German Americans, and came under the care of the Benedictine Abbacy of Muenster. In 1921, homesteader John Bunko donated the hill to the Abbacy as a place of pilgrimage.

In 1928, a large white marble statue of the Madonna and Child, made in Italy, was erected on the hill. In 1938 Antonio Molaro of Saskatoon designed and built the permanent chapel of local stone, and the next year the cairns that form the Stations of the Cross.

To Help You Plan Your Pilgrimage

Schedule: Pilgrimage day is the Feast of Our Lady of Mount Carmel, celebrated on the Sunday following July 16. The day begins with Reconciliation and Mass, followed by a picnic lunch and devotions to Our Lady. Later there is the Way of the Cross, Benediction, a procession with the Blessed Sacrament from the altar to the statue on the top of the hill, and finally the Blessing of the Sick.

For your convenience: St. Peter's Abbey in Muenster can accommodate guests, as can St. Ursula's Convent at Bruno. There are hotels and motels in the nearby towns and villages.

For further information: St. Peter's Abbey, P.O. Box 10, Muenster, SK S0K 2Y0.

Also of interest: Buildings of historical and religious interest include Muenster's St. Peter's Abbey and St. Peter's Cathedral (both with paintings by Berthold von Imhoff), and the Ursuline Convent in Bruno.

COLE BAY

Mary, Mother of God Shrine

Cole Bay is on Canoe Lake near Highway 903 in northwestern Saskatchewan.

The grotto has a wooden shelter in front of it. It was erected on the mission grounds by the Cree in 1981.

In June, Natives come on pilgrimage from all over the northland. The Saturday of the two-day pilgrimage includes Reconciliation, Mass and Blessing of the Sick, as well as hymns and testimonies in Cree. Sunday includes Mass, Benediction and Way of the Cross.

There are teepees for overnight camping. There is a canteen and a sale of religious articles.

CUDWORTH

Shrine of Our Lady of Sorrows

The shrine is on 20 acres of land, 3 kilometres southwest of Cudworth.

History

The shrine began when Ukrainians set up a wooden cross here to commemorate the hilltop where they had first gathered for prayer in the early and difficult years of pioneering. In 1948 the Stations of the Cross were added and soon a small chapel was built for a statue of Our Lady of Sorrows. In 1964 the old Church of St. Demetrius was moved and attached to the chapel.

The Shrine

Today there is a beautiful fieldstone sanctuary housing the white painted wooden crucifix with the statues of the Virgin Mary, Mary Magdalene and St. John. Away from the Calvary, in three different directions, you will find stone cairns. On top of the cairns are statues of the fifth, sixth and seventh angels from the Apocalypse of John.

To Help You Plan Your Pilgrimage

Schedule: There is an annual pilgrimage from Thursday to Sunday in the tenth week after Easter. The shrine is under the pastoral care of Holy Eucharist Ukrainian Catholic Church in Cudworth.

Also of interest: To the west on Highway 41 are the churches at Alvena and Smuts that have paintings by Stepan Meush. Not far away are the shrines at St. Laurent, Wakaw and Carmel. (See separate entries.)

DILLON

Grotto of Our Lady of Lourdes

Dillon is on Peter Pond Lake in northwestern Saskatchewan. It can be reached by Highways 155 and 925.

Around 1970, a light was seen on the lake in line with the present shrine site about 2 kilometres from Dillon. The land was cleared and the first Mass was celebrated in 1971. In 1982 the Lourdes Grotto with a shelter was built. The next year a 5-metre-high cross was erected.

Around the Feast of the Assumption (August 15), a three-day pilgrimage is held (one that includes singing in Chipewyan), also Reconciliation, Mass, Benediction and Stations of the Cross.

FILE HILLS RESERVE

Grotto to Kateri Tekakwitha

The grotto was built in 1987 to celebrate the Marian Year. In 1988 a Way of the Cross was added. This is a place of Cree and Sioux pilgrimage near Lebret. (See separate entry.)

FORGET

Shrine of Our Lady of La Salette

Forget is in the southeast corner of the province. It is 75 kilometres due east of Weyburn by Highway 13.

The first Catholic settlers in the area were francophones coming from Quebec, France and Belgium in the 1890s. In 1899 the La Salette Fathers arrived and built the first parish church. Annual pilgrimages to Our Lady of La Salette began in 1922 and continued until 1929. The depression years made it difficult for people to travel, but the pilgrimage was revived in 1954. An outdoor shrine was built of fieldstone and the grounds around it beautifully landscaped.

The shrine is open all year. Pilgrimage day varies from a Sunday in late May to a Sunday in early June.

ILE-À-LA-CROSSE

Shrine of the Immaculate Conception

Ile-à-la-Crosse is in northwestern Saskatchewan and can be reached by Highways 155 and 908.

The grotto was built in 1944 at the historic St. Jean-Baptiste Mission, not far from the church. Caravans of pilgrims on the way to Lac Ste. Anne, Alberta, used to stop here and camp. In the 1970s the shrine went into decline, but in 1984 it was revived.

To Help You Plan Your Pilgrimage

Schedule: The weekend closest to the Feast of St. John the Baptist (June 24) is pilgrimage time. On Saturday evening there is Reconciliation, prayers and Mass. On Sunday there is a procession from the church to the shrine, a Mass, a healing service and a final blessing. Liturgies are in Cree and English, Chipewyan and Métis.

KAPOSVAR

Shrine of Our Lady of Lourdes

Kaposvar is 5 kilometres south of Esterhazy, near the Manitoba border.

Kaposvar was founded by Count Paul Esterhazy, who brought Hungarian families to settle here in 1886. The first church was built of logs in 1892 and the present stone one in 1908. During 1941–42 the youth of the parish built the Shrine of Our Lady of Lourdes. The first pilgrimage took place in the Marian Year of 1954. A stone Stations of the Cross was built in 1986.

To Help You Plan Your Pilgrimage

Schedule: The annual pilgrimage is on the Feast of the Assumption, celebrated on the weekend after August 15. There is a monument on the site to the first Hungarian settlers and many old restored buildings.

For your convenience: There are hotels in Esterhazy.

For further information: Kaposvar Historic Site Society, P.O. Box 115, Esterhazy, SK S0A 0X0.

KRONAU

Shrine of Our Lady of Lourdes

Kronau is about a 30-minute drive southeast of Regina along Highway 33. Before you come to the village of Kronau, you will see the shrine sign beside the highway. Turn left and drive about 10 kilometres.

History

The Kronau area was settled in the late 19th and early 20th centuries by Germans from Russia. In 1913 Father H. Metzger, a native of France, took over the mission of St. Peter at Kronau. Inspired by the slope of the hill beside the church, he suggested that the parish build a grotto resembling Lourdes, France. In 1917 parishioners erected a grotto on the hill close to Many Bones Creek. Cut into the hillside, the fieldstone shrine contains an altar and pulpit.

To Help You Plan
Your Pilgrimage

Schedule: The shrine is accessible at all times, as is the church. Masses or services with lay presiders are held every Sunday. The annual pilgrimage is on the Feast of the Assumption (the second Sunday in August) with morning Mass, afternoon Marian devotions, Blessing of the Sick, Rosary and procession with the statue of Mary. Marian devotions are held at the grotto during the month of May.

For your convenience: Bed-and-breakfast with a farm family can be arranged.

For further information: St. Peter's Parish, Box 154, Kronau, SK S0G 2T0. ☎ (306) 885-2032; 🖳 (306) 885-2172.

LEBRET

Old Mission Stations of the Cross

Lebret is northeast of Regina, near Fort Qu'Appelle.

History

In the 19th century this was a stopover point for many of the best-known missionaries of the West. The first log chapel was built in 1866, and soon Lebret became the missionary centre for Métis and native peoples of southern Saskatchewan. Here Father Hugonard met with the famous chief Sitting Bull and later became a conciliator in the Rebellion of 1885.

Today there is a cairn marking the site of the Lebret Mission. Nearby is an illuminated cross marking the spot where a cross was first raised in 1865. There is a simple Stations of the Cross leading up a hill to an old chapel. From the hill there is a good view of the region. Sacred Heart Church in Lebret has Sunday morning Mass.

Also of interest: There is a shrine at the nearby File Hills Reserve. (See separate entry.)

LESTOCK

Shrine of Mary, Queen of Hearts

To get to Lestock from Regina, take Highway 6 north and turn east at Raymore. Lestock is about 45 kilometres east on Highway 15.

In the 1930s and 40s, parish priest Father J. A. Ménard encouraged novenas to Mary, Queen of All Hearts. In 1951 the parish name was changed to Mary, Queen of All Hearts. The first public pilgrimage was held during the 1954 Marian Year. In 1958 an outdoor shrine with an arched roof was built to hold an Italian-made sculpture of Mary.

To Help You Plan Your Pilgrimage

Schedule: The church is open during the year, though it no longer has a resident parish priest. Pilgrimage day is the first Sunday in June.

For further information: St. Stanislaus Church, P.O. Box 220, Ituna, SK S0A 1N0.

Also of interest: The shrines at Yorkton to the east and Rama to the north are nearby. (See separate entries.)

PONTEIX

Our Lady of Sorrows Shrine

Ponteix is in southwestern Saskatchewan. From Gravelbourg take Highways 58 south and 13 west.

History

The Parish of Notre-Dame d'Auvergne (Our Lady of Auvergne) was founded in 1908 by Father Albert Royer in this mainly French farming community. Father Royer had a friend, Canon Teytard, who lived in the region of Auvergne, France, and who collected church antiquities. When Father Royer indicated he was about to found a parish in honour of Mary, Canon Teytard gave him a 400-year-old oak statue of Our Lady of Sorrows. Originally covered in gold, the statue had been hidden by peasants in a haystack during the French Revolution to save it from desecration and vandalism.

The statue was the only thing to survive the fire that destroyed the Church of Our Lady of Auvergne in Ponteix in 1922. The present church, of fine Romanesque style with two square towers, was finished in 1930. In 1934, in the midst of the economic depression, the pilgrimages began. The shrine is now the place of pilgrimage for the Gravelbourg Diocese. The Feast of Our Lady of Mount Carmel (July 16) is pilgrimage day.

Also of interest: The cathedral in Gravelbourg with its wall and ceiling paintings by Msgr. Charles Maillard is worth a visit.

RAMA

Grotto of Our Lady of Lourdes

The grotto is on Highway 5, about 45 kilometres northwest of Canora in eastern Saskatchewan. It is next to the Church of St. Anthony.

History

In 1933, Oblate Father Anthony Sylla was appointed first permanent pastor and he began planning the grotto with his Polish and Ukrainian parishioners. Construction began on the very day that Germany invaded Poland in 1939.

The next year an entranceway and semicircular wall were built and the first pilgrimage was held in 1941. Later, grottoes were added with the Crucifixion, Descent from the Cross, Entombment and Resurrection of Jesus. In 1954 the Knights of Columbus donated a statue of Our Lady of Grace and built an artificial lake. In the late 1950s the Stations of the Cross were built. There is a miniature replica of the parish church with a guest register in it.

To Help You Plan Your Pilgrimage

Schedule: The grotto is open all day from May 1 to October 30. Guided tours can be arranged. The Catholic Women's League sponsors the Rosary during the summer months. The Feast of the Assumption (August 15) begins on the evening of August 14, with Mass at the grotto, the living rosary and a candlelight procession around the grounds and into the church. The Blessed Sacrament is exposed for adoration all night. The next morning the first of several Masses begins, culminating in a solemn Mass. The Way of the Cross and pilgrims' consecration to Mary are held in the afternoon. The pilgrimage ends with Benediction of the Blessed Sacrament and the Blessing of the Sick.

For your convenience: Accommodations can be found in Rama and the nearby communities.

For further information: Archdiocese of Regina ☎ (306) 352-1651.

Also of interest: In Rama, visit Saints Peter and Paul Ukrainian Catholic Church with its onion domes. Canora has a heritage Ukrainian Orthodox church in the Kiev style.

REWARD

Holy Rosary Shrine

Reward is due west of Saskatoon, close to the Alberta border. Take Route 14 west and turn south on Route 675.

History

St. Joseph Colony was established as a new area for settlement in 1905 when Saskatchewan became a province of Canada. Many Catholic German Russians came and settled at Reward in this colony.

Berthold Von Imhoff was asked to do paintings of the fifteen Mysteries of the Rosary for the Church of the Holy Rosary. Imhoff, born and trained in Germany, completed his works in 1920. In 1932, when the German Russians asked for a pilgrimage place for their colony, Holy Rosary Church was chosen because of its importance in the community and because of its central location. A shrine to Our Lady of the Rosary was set up in the church.

The Shrine

In 1963 a new parish church was built, but the old one was retained for pilgrimages. It was completely renovated during the Holy Year of 1975. Now a provincial historic site, it is open from mid-June to mid-September.

Pilgrimage day is the Sunday closest to July 16 (Our Lady of Mount Carmel).

SASKATOON

Our Lady of the Prairies Shrine

This shrine is located in Holy Spirit Church, 114 Kingsmere Place. It was opened in 1983 during the national convention of the Catholic Women's League.

History

The shrine celebrates the influence of Mary among the people of Canada's wheat province. In 1933 the Catholic bishops of the province consecrated Saskatchewan to Mary, Queen of the Holy Rosary. In 1957 J. P. Leier started Our Lady of the Prairies Foundation to carry out religious, educational and charitable works among the people. The shrine was one of the Foundation's projects.

The Shrine

The statue of Our Lady of the Prairies was designed by New York artist Robert Rambusch and cast in bonded bronze in Florence, Italy. Mary carries a sheaf of wheat instead of a baby. The wheat symbolizes not only Saskatchewan life but Jesus Christ, the bread of life.

The backdrop for the statue is a mural created by New York artist Ronald Millard. In paintings and carved wood reliefs, it illustrates nine of the most important places of Marian pilgrimage in Saskatchewan.

To Help You Plan Your Pilgrimage

Schedule: The annual pilgrimage day is the Feast of the Birth of Mary (September 8).

For further information: Our Lady of the Prairies Foundation, 2317 Ewart Avenue, Saskatoon, SK S7J 1Y3.

Also of interest: The Cathedral of St. Paul is on Spadina Crescent. In the chapel of St. Thomas More College is a mural by William Kurelek. The many-domed Ukrainian Catholic Cathedral of St. George has several paintings by Theodore Baran.

Shrine of Our Lady of Good Counsel

The shrine is on the grounds of the retreat centre called Queen's House. Our Lady of Good Counsel is patroness of the Catholic Women's League of Canada, and members from the Diocese of Saskatoon had the shrine built in 1965.

ST. LAURENT

Our Lady of Lourdes Shrine

St. Laurent is on the North Saskatchewan River, a few kilometres east of Duck Lake. Duck Lake is on Highway 11, halfway between Prince Albert and Saskatoon.

History

St. Laurent had been a camping ground for Natives and Métis. A priest regularly accompanied them on the buffalo hunt. In 1879 Oblate Brother Jean Piquet, originally from the area of Lourdes, France, arrived. Noticing the spring and the similarity of the land to Lourdes, he began the shrine. The first cure occurred in 1884 after a novena, and resulted in the first *ex-voto*, a large statue of Our Lady of Lourdes.

The colony prospered until the Northwest Rebellion broke out. Oblate Father Vital Fourmand, who ran the mission, was arrested along with many other priests of the area. The mission buildings narrowly escaped being put to the torch. The whole population of St. Laurent fled, never to return. The mission limped along for a few years after the rebellion, but it never recovered.

The shrine, however, continued to prosper. The first interparish pilgrimage was organized in 1905. In the late 1930s a log church was built to commemorate the old mission. After it burned in 1990, it was replaced with a modern church in the shape of a teepee.

The Shrine

The Grotto of Our Lady of Lourdes is in a building that is open on one side. In front of it is a shed-like structure that has seating for several thousand pilgrims. There is a Way of the Cross and a Rosary arch on the grounds. The original spring is still there and pilgrims take the water home in bottles.

To Help You Plan Your Pilgrimage

Schedule: The shrine is open from June to September. The Feast of Our Lady of Mount Carmel (July 16) includes a torchlight procession. There is a preparatory novena. The Feast of the Assumption is celebrated on August 15. On the evening before each feast there is usually a Stations of the Cross by candlelight. Some pilgrims hold an all-night vigil at the grotto. In the morning there are Masses in French, English and several Aboriginal languages. In the afternoon there is a special Mass celebrated by the Bishop of Prince Albert, followed by a procession of the Blessed Sacrament and a Blessing of the Sick. During the pilgrimage there is always a peace pipe ceremony and sometimes drumming and singing by the Beardy Cree Singers. In the summer months there are Masses every Sunday afternoon.

For your convenience: During the pilgrimages there is a food booth on the grounds. There are stores and restaurants in nearby Duck Lake. There is camping on the shrine grounds. There are hotels and motels at Duck Lake and Rosthern.

For further information: Our Lady of Lourdes Shrine, St. Laurent de Grandin, P.O. Box 187, Duck Lake, SK S0K 1J0.

Also of interest: The rectory by the shrine is historic. The cemetery contains the graves of many Métis killed in the Northwest Rebellion. There are history museums at Duck Lake, Fort Carlton and Batoche. The grave of Gabriel Dumont is in the cemetery at Batoche.

ST. WALBURG

Shrine of Our Lady of Lourdes

St. Walburg is northwest of North Battleford. Take Highways 4 and 26.

In 1980, to celebrate the 75th anniversary of Saskatchewan's entrance into Confederation, the Parish of Our Lady of the Assumption decided to replace a tiny shrine from the 1950s with a full-sized grotto. It was blessed by Bishop Morin of Prince Albert in 1981. There is a Stations of the Cross here.

To Help You Plan Your Pilgrimage

Schedule: The annual pilgrimage is on the weekend nearest to the Feast of the Assumption (August 15). It begins Saturday evening with Mass in the church, a candlelight procession to the grotto, and the Litany of Loreto. On Sunday afternoon at the grotto, there are the Stations of the Cross, Mass, Benediction, a Blessing of the Sick and a procession of the Blessed Sacrament back to the church. The pilgrimage ends with a giant campfire.

Also of interest: Assumption Church has paintings by Berthold von Imhoff. The local art gallery contains 200 of his works and the church at Paradise Hill has 18 of his panels.

WAKAW

Shrine of St. Theresa

Wakaw is about 80 kilometres northeast of Saskatoon by Highway 41.

This shrine is in the Church of St. Theresa of Lisieux and is the national shrine of this saint. Theresa was canonized in 1925. Her spirituality centres on the meaning of Christ's charity – love of neighbour.

To Help You Plan Your Pilgrimage

Schedule: Pilgrimage days are the second Sunday of June and the first Sunday after the Feast of Theresa of the Child Jesus (October 1). Each pilgrimage day is preceded by a novena. On pilgrimage day there is a procession and Mass. There is plenty of parking, and there are religious articles for sale.

For further information: Shrine of St. Theresa, P.O. Box 795, Wakaw, SK S0K 4P0. ☎ (306) 422-8531; 🖳 (306) 422-8586.

WOLLASTON LAKE

Grotto of Our Lady of Lourdes

Wollaston Lake is in the far northeast of the province. Highway 905 comes to the other side of the lake but not to this community.

Around 1980, before electricity was available, the community gathered in the coffee shop (which had its own electric generator) to see an old movie, *The Song of Bernadette.* Five women were so affected by this movie that they persuaded the parish priest, who was from France, to take them to Lourdes. Because of their experience there, they decided to build a small grotto on their return home. The villagers joined them and built it in front of St. Adrien's Church. In 1981 it was blessed by Archbishop Dumouchel.

Schedule: The annual pilgrimage is on July 12 to 14 and includes Masses, Rosary, Way of the Cross and many social gatherings. Liturgies are in Chipewyan and English.

YORKTON

Shrine of Our Lady of Perpetual Help

Yorkton is near the Manitoba border, northeast of Regina.

History

Ukrainian settlement in the Yorkton area began in 1902. The Yorkton Mission was begun by Belgian Redemptorist Father Achille Delaere, who adopted the Ukrainian Rite and built the first church in 1910. Four years later the present Church of Our Lady of Perpetual Help was built. The mission also included a monastery, convent, several Ukrainian schools and a printing press.

In 1916 a hand-painted icon of Our Mother of Perpetual Help was installed and the pilgrimages began. Between 1939 and 1941, artist Stepan Meush decorated the dome of the church. From 1954 to 1955 the church was enlarged to its present size.

The Shrine

The Church of Our Lady of Perpetual Help is a large building in the Byzantine style with barrel-vaulted roofs and a dome over the crossing of the nave and transept. The sanctuary is under the dome so that worshippers can follow services from three sides.

At the base of the altar are 28 statuettes of Byzantine-rite saints. Behind the altar is the large icon of Our Mother of Perpetual Help painted by Igor Suhacev in 1964. It is framed by a wooden screen or rizba, designed by Suhacev and carved by Warren Smith.

The painting on the inside of the dome is 19 metres in diameter and is unique in Canada. Artist Stepan Meush was trained in Lviv, Western Ukraine, and in Italy. Here he uses the fresco method and many perspective techniques of the baroque ceiling painters. The subject is the Coronation of the Virgin. In the many circles of clouds are 157 angels.

The four evangelists on the pendentives of the dome were painted by Redemptorist Father Metzger, and there are paintings by various artists in other parts of the church. On the grounds is a Grotto of Our Lady of Lourdes.

To Help You Plan Your Pilgrimage

Schedule: The shrine is locked except during liturgies. During daily office hours, the receptionist will admit visitors to view the shrine. Pilgrimage is on the Sunday before the July 1st weekend and is preceded by a three-day mission. For schedules of Divine Liturgy, youth liturgy, healing liturgy, May *Moleben* and other Marian feasts, please write.

For your convenience: There are hotels, motels and restaurants in Yorkton.

For further information: Our Lady of Perpetual Help Parish, 155 Catherine Street, Yorkton, SK S3N 0B9. ☎ (306) 783-4594; 🖳 (306) 782-4214.

Also of interest: St. Joseph's College has an interesting chapel. There are many fascinating Ukrainian churches in the Yorkton area, including the modern Church of the Sacred Heart at Ituna, with paintings by Roman Kowel, and the Church of Saints Peter and Paul at Canora.

Alberta

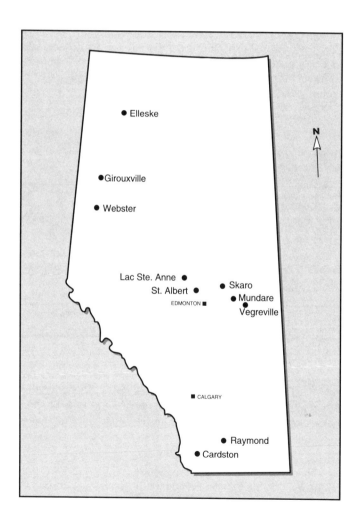

- Elleske
- Girouxville
- Webster
- Lac Ste. Anne
- St. Albert
- Skaro
- Mundare
- EDMONTON
- Vegreville
- CALGARY
- Raymond
- Cardston

N

CARDSTON

Grotto of Our Lady of the Rockies

The grotto is on the Blood Indian Reserve, 12 kilometres northwest of Cardston. It stands in front of the Church of the Immaculate Conception, a church with an interesting stepped facade.

A Way of the Cross leads from the church to the grotto. Pilgrimage day celebrates the Feast of the Body and Blood of Christ (Corpus Christi) and usually occurs in early June. On that day there is a procession and outdoor Mass. During the summer months, Masses are occasionally celebrated at the grotto.

For further information: Saint Theresa Parish, P.O. Box 788, Cardston, AB T0K 0K0. ☎ (403) 653-3201.

Also of interest: The mountains of Waterton Lakes National Park are just west of here.

ELLESKE

Shrine of Notre-Dame-de-Lourdes

Elleske is in northern Alberta between Fort Vermillion and High Level. This grotto is on a Beaver Indian Reserve. Pilgrimage day varies but it is usually in July.

GIROUXVILLE

Notre-Dame-de-Lourdes Shrine

Girouxville is in the Peace River country in northwestern Alberta. From Edmonton take Highway 43 to Donnelly, then Route 49 west 15 kilometres, then Route 744 north 2 kilometres to Girouxville. This region is the most northern grain-growing area in North America.

History

The Parish of Notre-Dame-de-Lourdes was founded in 1928 by the remarkable Oblate missionary Bishop Emile Grouard. A native of France, Grouard was given a special statue of Our

Lady of Lourdes by the Bishop of Lourdes, France, in 1928. However, the outdoor shrine was not established until 1942, eleven years after Grouard's death. The shrine is on the grounds of the church.

To Help You Plan Your Pilgrimage

Schedule: The shrine is open every day. Pilgrimage day is the Feast of the Assumption (August 15). On that day there is a Mass, Blessing of the Sick and Stations of the Cross. In early September there is another pilgrimage with a candlelight procession and Marian devotions.

For further information: Notre-Dame-de-Lourdes Church, P.O. Box 298, Falher, AB T0H 1M0 ☎ (780) 323-4290.

Also of interest: The Girouxville Museum is interesting and at Grouard are the St. Bernard Mission Church and the grave of Bishop Grouard.

LAC STE. ANNE

Shrine of Ste. Anne

The shrine is 60 kilometres northwest of Edmonton. Take the Trans-Canada Highway west and turn onto Highway 43 at Manly Corner. Turn onto Route 33 at the sign to Alberta Beach. Follow the sign that says Mission.

The shrine is unusual among Canadian shrines in that over 90 percent of the pilgrims are native people and most of these pilgrims camp out.

History

In 1843 Father Jean-Baptiste Thibault blessed Devil's Lake and renamed it Lac Ste. Anne. There were delays in creating a permanent mission here because the Hudson's Bay Company opposed the missionaries who wanted to teach the Métis and Indians farming methods, thus jeopardizing the fur trade. But soon Lac Ste. Anne became the base for evangelizing the northwest – by horseback in summer and by dog team in winter. Father Lacombe also worked here.

In 1861, when Bishop Taché of St. Boniface decided to move the centre of the missions to St. Albert, Lac Ste. Anne declined. In 1887 Oblate Father Jean-Marie Lestanc left Lac Ste. Anne to visit his native Brittany after an absence of 30 years.

While there he went to the shrine of Ste. Anne d'Auray and came back with the motivation to rekindle devotion to the grandmother of Jesus at Lac Ste. Anne. By 1889 a larger church had been built and a pilgrimage was organized. The donation of a statue of Ste. Anne, the support of Bishop Grandin of St. Albert, and the report of cures all helped the pilgrimage to grow in the 1890s.

In 1935 a new wooden shrine able to accommodate 2,000 people was completed. This shrine was used until the 1980s when Father Paul Hudon completely redesigned the grounds and built the present modern buildings.

The Shrine

The main shrine to Ste. Anne is like a gigantic shed with a triangular profile and a triangular floor plan. Its sides are open to the weather and only the sanctuary area is fully enclosed. Here a Gothic wooden shrine houses the statue of Ste. Anne above the altar. This building can seat 3,000 people and can accommodate another 1,000 people standing.

Away from the shrine toward the sacred water area is a series of cedar-shingled triangular huts holding the Stations of the Cross painted by Native artist Alex Twinn. A bronze Calvary group south of the shrine is on a stone terrace reached by six steps. Nearby is a wooden building in the shape of a teepee. Inside is a circle of eight reconciliation rooms for confession in English, French, Blackfoot, Inuit and four other aboriginal languages.

The entrance to the grounds is marked by a large wooden cross. Across the road from it is the old parish church, which was once a dance hall. Opposite the rectory is a stone cairn supporting a statue of Ste. Anne and the child Mary. On the side of the cairn is a government plaque commemorating the first Catholic mission in Alberta.

The most surprising thing about the shrine grounds is that around the Feast of Ste. Anne it is like a giant campground with thousands of people coming from all over Canada and the United States to meet old friends and renew cultural ties. During the pilgrimage there is a procession down to the water's edge. A bishop goes out on the lake and blesses the water. Then the crowd wades in to bathe in the health-giving water. Many take water home in bottles.

To Help You Plan Your Pilgrimage

Schedule: The shrine is accessible from May until the end of August. Almost all pilgrims come here for the five-day Feast of Ste. Anne in the third week of July for Masses, confession and a candlelight procession.

For information on liturgies in Dogrib, Blackfoot and Cree, veneration of the relic, Blessing of the Sick, processions, Way of the Cross, Rosary, youth tent, Bible study, and many cultural events, please write.

For your convenience: Camping is free on the grounds but there are no hook-ups for trailers and campers. There are campgrounds at Wabamun, Stony Plain and Spruce Grove, and hotels in Edmonton. During the celebrations there are several food concessions on the grounds and a small restaurant. In the nearby community of Alberta Beach there are several restaurants and grocery stores. During the celebrations a store for religious articles and souvenirs is open. There are information boards and washrooms around the grounds.

For further information: Ste. Anne Parish, P.O. Box 118, Lac Ste. Anne, AB T0E 0A0. ☎ (780) 924-2381; 🖷 (780) 924-2249.

Also of interest: St. Albert has a grotto and an old Catholic mission. Edmonton has St. Joseph's Basilica. (See separate entry.) South of Edmonton, at the Hobbema Reserve, is the Church of Our Lady of Seven Sorrows in the shape of a teepee. It contains Alex Twinn's series of windows on the life of Christ showing Christ as a Native person.

MUNDARE

Grotto "Golgotha of Mundare"
Mundare is about 70 kilometres east of Edmonton by the Trans-Canada Highway.

History
Mundare is important in the history of Ukrainian Catholic settlement in Western Canada. In 1902 the Basilian Fathers and the Sisters Servants of Mary Immaculate arrived at Beaver Lake, just southeast of Mundare, to work among the Ukrainian immigrants who had been settling there for over a decade. Because

of the railway Mundare was growing rapidly, so they decided to build their main church here in 1910. In 1922 the Basilians built a monastery here as a centre for their mission churches in east-central Alberta.

The Shrine

In 1933 a hill was built near the monastery to resemble Mount Calvary and to celebrate the 1900th anniversary of redemption. The 14 Stations of the Cross lead through trimmed hedges and vines to the top of the hill. In 1938, the 950th anniversary of the Baptism of Ukraine was celebrated with the building of a 17-metre metal cross on the summit. It is illuminated at night.

To Help You Plan Your Pilgrimage

Schedule: The grotto is accessible at all times. The pilgrimage day is the Sunday nearest to the Feast of Saints Peter and Paul (June 29). On that day Divine Liturgy (Byzantine Rite) is celebrated in the grotto. This is followed by an outdoor meal in nearby Ukraina Park, and other religious functions, sports and games.

For your convenience: There are accommodations at Vegreville, east on Highway 16.

For further information: Saints Peter and Paul Parish, P.O. Box 379, Mundare, AB T0B 3H0. ☎ (780) 764-3860; ✉ (780) 764-3961 (monastery).

Also of interest: The present Church of Saints Peter and Paul has a series of frescoes by painter Mykola Denysenko. There is also a painted copy of the miraculous icon of the Mother of God venerated in the Basilian Monastery of Pochaiv, Ukraine, since 1597. The Basilians also have a new Ukrainian museum here.

RAYMOND

Shrine of Our Blessed Mother

Raymond is southeast of Lethbridge. The shrine is 5 kilometres south and 2 kilometres east of Raymond on the Kaupp family farm at New Dayton. The shrine is unusual in that it is on a private farm.

A 1987 Christmas gift of a statue of the Virgin Mary proved to be too big for the living room, so the solution was an outdoor shrine. The shrine was blessed in May 1988. The family made the little shrine available for the local parish's closing Mass of the Marian Year on the Feast of the Assumption. Since then the number of visitors continues to increase.

Schedule: The annual pilgrimage day is the Feast of the Assumption (August 15).

For further information: Sacred Heart Church, P.O. Box 278, Raymond, AB T0K 2S0.

SKARO

Grotto to Mary
Skaro is a rural community near Lamont by Highway 45, about 70 kilometres northeast of Edmonton.

History
In 1918 Father Sylla, pastor of the Polish Parish of Our Lady of Good Counsel, proposed a grotto. Father Philip Ruh, the first Ukrainian Rite Oblate in Canada, designed it. It was finished the following year and the pilgrimages began. In 1963 the present modern parish church was constructed. In 1966 the shrine celebrated the millennium of Christianity in Poland. In 1987 the first liturgy to launch the Marian Year in the Archdiocese of Edmonton was celebrated by Archbishop MacNeil at the Skaro shrine.

The Shrine
The grotto is on the grounds of the church. It is built of fieldstone on the side of a small hill, with tall evergreen trees behind it. In the cave of the grotto is an altar. On either side of the grotto are staircases that lead to a Calvary at the top.

The modern brick church has a square bell-tower and a niche with a statue of Our Lady of Good Counsel over the entrance. Inside are Gothic altarpieces with gold-ground panels of saints. In the centre of the main altarpiece is a picture of Our Lady of Good Counsel by artist Berthold von Imhoff.

To Help You Plan Your Pilgrimage

Schedule: The church is open all year, but the grotto is open only during the warmer months. Pilgrimage days are the Feast of the Assumption (August 15). On August 14, in the evening, there are confessions, Rosary and Vespers (in Polish) followed by a Solemn Mass and Procession of the Blessed Sacrament at the grotto. On August 15, in the morning, there is a Mass in the church, and a Mass for the sick at the grotto. The pilgrimage ends before noon with a Mass (in Polish) and a Procession of the Blessed Sacrament at the grotto. A Mass is celebrated every second Sunday (1st, 3rd, 5th) at Our Lady of Good Counsel Church.

For your convenience: On August 15 some meals are prepared by parishioners and the Catholic Women's League. There are restaurants and hotels in nearby towns such as Lamont.

For further information: Call (780) 895-7519 or contact Our Lady of the Angels, 10004–101 St., Fort Saskatchewan, AB T8L 1V9. ☎ (780) 998-3288.

ST. ALBERT

Our Lady of Lourdes Grotto
St. Albert is just northwest of Edmonton. Take the St. Albert Trail. The Grotto of Our Lady of Lourdes is on the grounds of the old mission of the Oblates of Mary Immaculate. The mission is the highest point in St. Albert and you can see it on your left as you drive north from Edmonton.

History
In 1861 the St. Albert Mission was founded by Bishop Taché of St. Boniface and Father Lacombe, the famous missionary. The mission became the site of Alberta's first farms and its first hospital.

In 1870 St. Albert was made an episcopal see and Oblate Father Vital Grandin became the new bishop. He died in 1902; 10 years later the episcopal see was transferred to Edmonton.

The Shrine
At the entrance to the grounds is a statue of Father Lacombe holding up a crucifix. Immediately to the right is the original log chapel in which Father Lacombe lived and conducted his mission.

Next to this is the original four-storey mission that served as the third residence and headquarters of Bishop Grandin. Built between 1882 and 1887, it was in its earliest days a sort of community centre. Inside the building are Grandin's chapel and several exhibition rooms.

In the centre of the grounds is the Church of St. Albert. The crypt was built in 1900 to support a future cathedral. In 1922 the present parish church was built over the crypt instead. The crypt can be entered from the outside at the northeast side of the church. Inside is the tomb of the Venerable Bishop Grandin, whose cause for beatification was introduced in Rome in 1938. His tomb is flanked by the tombs of Father Lacombe and Father Leduc. Around the walls are showcases on the lives of Grandin and Brother Anthony Kowalczyk.

Within sight of the crypt door is the outdoor Grotto of Our Lady of Lourdes. The first grotto was built by Oblate brothers and seminarians in 1920 and the first annual pilgrimage was organized in 1938. In 1955 a larger grotto was constructed using stones of the original one. It has a niche with an altar for Mass and there is an outdoor pulpit in front of the grotto. The open space in front of the grotto is flanked on both sides by the Stations of the Cross, consisting of white plaques embedded in cairns made of stones from the old grotto.

To Help You Plan Your Pilgrimage

Schedule: The Grotto of Our Lady of Lourdes and the Stations are accessible in spring, summer and fall. The annual pilgrimage is held on the Sunday closest to August 15, the Feast of the Assumption. Masses are celebrated in the church on Saturday evenings and on Sundays.

For your convenience: There is parking on the grounds. Brochures and books are available at the centre. Everything is accessible to the handicapped. Hotels and restaurants can be found in St. Albert or Edmonton.

For further information: 7 St. Vital Ave., St. Albert, AB T8N 1K1. ☎ (780) 459-6691; 🖷 (780) 459-6679; e-mail: st_alb@telusplanet.net.

Also of interest: Morinville has the historic St-Jean-Baptiste Church. Edmonton's Basilica of St. Joseph on Jasper Avenue is the largest church in the region. If you are in Red Deer be sure to see St. Mary's Church, the little masterpiece of Aboriginal architect Douglas Cardinal. The shrine of Lac Ste. Anne is to the northwest of Edmonton. (See separate entry.)

VEGREVILLE

Shrine of Our Lady of the Highway

Vegreville is about 90 kilometres east of Edmonton on the Yellowhead Highway (No. 16). The shrine is on the eastern outskirts of town.

The Shrine

This is a wayside shrine built by the Knights of Columbus for the weary traveller. It is an outdoor area enclosed by spruce trees. At the centre is a circular concrete platform with a statue of Our Lady of the Highway in Carrara marble. Around the platform is a Stations of the Cross.

To Help You Plan Your Pilgrimage

Schedule: There is no pilgrimage day. On the Sunday of the Victoria Day weekend in May there is an evening Rosary followed by Benediction of the Blessed Sacrament.

For your convenience: There is parking by the grounds.

For further information: Holy Trinity Parish, P.O. Box 248, Vegreville, AB T0B 4L0.

Also of interest: Vegreville is notable for its giant aluminum pysanka (Easter egg) that rotates on a concrete and steel base. In July Vegreville hosts a Ukrainian Pysanka Festival. The Mundare and Skaro shrines are not far away to the northwest. (See separate entries.)

WEBSTER

Shrine of Our Lady of Czestochowa

Webster is a farming community 40 kilometres north of Grand Prairie in northwestern Alberta. This is a small Polish shrine that is open all year. Pilgrimage day is the Feast of the Assumption (August 15).

British Columbia

CACHE CREEK

Immaculate Heart of Mary Shrine

The shrine is east of Cache Creek by the Trans-Canada Highway and north on Highway 97.

The Shrine

The shrine was founded in 1988 by Bishop Sabatini of the Diocese of Kamloops as a Marian Year project. It is surrounded by dry hills and desert scenery. The chapel, designed by Doug Huggins, is in the shape of a trihedron. Inside is a beautiful wooden statue of Mary of the Immaculate Heart, principal patroness of the diocese.

There is an altar for indoor Masses for groups of 100 or less. Around the entrance to the chapel is an enclosed semicircular compound for outdoor celebrations. Around the semicircle are 14 niches with bronze and wood plaques of the Stations of the Cross. On the grounds is a Grotto of Our Lady of Lourdes.

To Help You Plan Your Pilgrimage

Schedule: The shrine is open from September to June during regular office hours. It is closed in July and August. There is a pilgrimage on the Feast of the Immaculate Heart of Mary.

For your convenience: There are motels and restaurants around Cache Creek. In the spring of 1992 a renewal centre opened at the shrine and can accommodate pilgrims.

For further information: Shrine of the Immaculate Heart of Mary, P.O. Box 250, Cache Creek, BC V0K 1H0. ☎ (250) 457-9930; 🖳 (250) 457-9206.

Also of interest: The Bonaparte Church is located on a nearby Native reserve. At Vernon is the O'Keefe Ranch, which was one of British Columbia's largest ranches at the turn of the century. On it is tiny St. Ann's Church, built by rancher Cornelius O'Keefe in 1887 and served by travelling Oblate priests.

DELTA

Shrine of Our Mother of Consolation

Delta, as its name implies, is on low-lying land at the mouth of the Fraser River. From downtown Vancouver it can be reached by the Vancouver–Blaine Freeway. The shrine is at 3900 Arthur Drive, Ladner.

History

In 1943 the Augustinian Order took over an abandoned diocesan seminary and transformed it into their monastery. They built a small chapel that seated 80 and named it for Our Mother of Consolation. It is in the Tudor style with natural oak. Inside is a statue of Our Mother of Consolation.

To Help You Plan Your Pilgrimage

Schedule: The shrine has no pilgrimages but it is open all year. There are daily Masses; devotions are personal.

For your convenience: There are accommodations 5 kilometres away in Tsawwassen. The nearby parish is the Church of the Sacred Heart of Jesus.

For further information: Sacred Heart Parish, P.O. Box 10, Delta, BC V4K 3N5.

FORT ST. JAMES

Our Lady of the Assumption Grotto

Fort St. James is about 160 kilometres northwest of Prince George. Take Highway 16 west to Vanderhoof, then Highway 27 north. The grotto is at Camp Morice, 8 kilometres from the town.

History

Fort St. James was established in 1806 by explorer Simon Fraser as part of the Northwest Company's expansion west of the Rocky Mountains. Itinerant priests arrived at the fort at irregular intervals, but the Oblates opened their first permanent mission in 1867 at the request of the local Indian chief.

The Shrine

Built in 1981 in thanksgiving for all the frontier missionaries, nurses, teachers and others who came to work here, the grotto is on the spot where the first missionaries set up camp.

To Help You Plan Your Pilgrimage

Schedule: Local pilgrimage day is the Sunday nearest to the Feast of the Assumption (August 15). On that day there is the Rosary followed by a Mass. After the celebration there is a meal for hundreds of people.

For your convenience: There are cabins on the property and motels in Fort St. James.

For further information: Our Lady of the Assumption Grotto, Camp Morice, P.O. Box 877, Fort St. James, BC V0J 1P0.

Also of interest: The Gothic Church of Our Lady of Good Hope, built in 1872 at Stuart Lake, is the second oldest Catholic church in British Columbia. Behind it is the workshop where Father Morice, a remarkable pioneer and missionary from France, ran a printing press. The old log chapel at Pinchi, just north of Fort St. James, is still maintained by the Natives.

MISSION

Shrine of Our Lady of Lourdes

Mission is in the Fraser River Valley, about 60 kilometres east of Vancouver on Highway 7.

The municipality originated with the founding of St. Mary's Mission by Oblate Father Leon Fouquet in 1860. Eventually a residential school for the native people was built and in 1892 a domed shrine to Our Lady of Lourdes was built. Because vandalism made the shrine unsafe in 1965, it had to be taken down. Presently, plans are being made to build a replica.

Today the shrine grounds sit on a hill overlooking the Fraser River and the Fraser River Heritage Park.

To Help You Plan Your Pilgrimage

Schedule: The shrine is open from 2:00 p.m. to 4:00 p.m. from May 1 to September 30. There is an annual local pilgrimage. The date, chosen by St. Joseph's Parish, varies from year to year.

For further information: Shrine of Our Lady of Lourdes, St. Joseph's Parish, 32550–7th Avenue, Mission, BC V2V 2B9. ☎ and 🖳 (604) 826-5887.

Also of interest: The graves of the pioneer Oblates are in the Fraser River Heritage Park along with the ruins of St. Mary's Mission. On Mount Mary-Ann is the Benedictine Abbey of Christ the King, whose modern bell-tower dominates the landscape.

VANCOUVER

Shrine of St. Jude

The shrine is at 3078 Renfrew Street. There is a spectacular view of the coastal mountains from the church.

History

St. Jude's Parish was first established in 1944 to accommodate the many servicemen returning from World War II who were building new homes in the area. The parish was named by its first pastor, Father Donald Campbell, who had made a novena to St. Jude for a particularly hopeless case and promised to name his first parish after this saint. In 1959 the parishioners requested and received a weekly novena to St. Jude. The next year the parish became an officially designated shrine and received a relic from Rome.

The Shrine
The present church was finished in 1964 in a modern style with cast concrete roof. In the sanctuary, the altar, altar platform and tabernacle stand are made of Mexican marble of an unusual grey burgundy colour. The altar contains the relics of St. Francis of Assisi and of the Japanese Martyrs.

The Shrine of St. Jude is in the northeast corner of the church. The floor is of Mexican marble. The hand-carved wooden statue of St. Jude and that of Our Lady on the opposite side are from Italy. There are some beautiful stained glass windows specially made for the shrine. The reliquary is mounted on a marble stand and placed behind opaque glass. A large painting of a scene from the life of St. Jude hangs on the wall.

On the church property is the Convent of the Missionary Sisters of Christ the King. In the school compound adjoining the convent is a Marian grotto.

To Help You Plan Your Pilgrimage

Schedule: The shrine is open all year. Every Wednesday evening there is a novena to St. Jude beginning with Mass at 7:30 p.m. and ending with the veneration of the relic. There is a special novena to St. Jude (October 20-28) prior to the Feast of St. Jude.

For your convenience: There is parking by the shrine. The shrine is equipped for the handicapped. There is a picnic area in John Henry Park.

For further information: St. Jude's Shrine, 3078 Renfrew Street (at 15th Ave.), Vancouver, BC V5M 3K6. ☎ (604) 434-6700; ✉ (604) 434-6799.

Also of interest: St. Mary's Church in Vancouver has a little Shrine of the Miraculous Medal. Holy Rosary Cathedral is in the Gothic style with double spires.

Northwest Territories

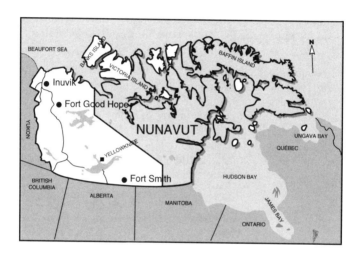

FORT SMITH

Grotto of Our Lady of Lourdes

Fort Smith is south of Great Slave Lake, near the Alberta border. The Fort was established by the Hudson Bay Company in 1874 as a shipping point for the Slave River Valley. In 1876 it became a bishop's see.

The large fieldstone Grotto of Our Lady of Lourdes was built in 1955 through the initiative of Father Joseph Adams. At that time practically the whole community turned out to build it.

Also of interest: St. Joseph's Cathedral, finished in 1960, is worth a visit. Not far away is the huge Wood Buffalo Park.

The northern native peoples, largely due to the great distances between settlements in the Northland, do not build shrines as much as the more southerly tribes. There are a few scattered grottoes, such as the one at Paulatuk on the Arctic Ocean. There are unusual churches such as Our Lady of Good Hope at Fort Good Hope and the igloo-shaped Our Lady of Victory at Inuvik.

Appendix

A PILGRIM'S LIST OF FACTS

Patron Saints of Pilgrims
- James the Greater
- Catherine of Alexandria

Patron Saints of Canada
- Joseph (since 1624)
- Anne

Largest Shrines in Canada
- St. Joseph's Oratory, Montreal, receives over 2,000,000 visitors every year.
- Ste. Anne de Beaupré receives around 1,500,000 visitors every year. It is probably the best known internationally.
- Our Lady of the Cape receives close to 1,000,000 visitors annually.
- The Hermitage of St. Anthony of Padua at Lac Bouchette receives up to 300,000 visitors every year.
- The Shrine of the Canadian Martyrs at Midland receives over 200,000 visitors annually.
  (Source: Survey of the Canadian Conference of Catholic Bishops and individual reports from the shrines.)

Canadian Saints Who Have Shrines
- St. Marguerite Bourgeoys – at the Notre Dame Motherhouse and at Notre-Dame-de-Bon-Secours in Montreal.
- St. Marguerite d'Youville – at the Grey Nuns' Motherhouse in Montreal and at Varennes.
- The Canadian Martyrs (Jean de Brébeuf, Gabriel Lalemant, Isaac Jogues, Anthony Daniel, Charles Garnier, Noël Chabanel, René Goupil and Jean de Lalande) – at Midland, Ontario and in Quebec City.

Canadian Shrines Dedicated to St. Anne

- Grotto of St. Ann, Outer Cove, Newfoundland
- Shrine of St. Ann, Chapel Island, Cape Breton, Nova Scotia
- St. Ann, Lennox Island, Prince Edward Island
- Ste-Anne-du-Bocage, Caraquet, New Brunswick
- Ste-Anne-de-Madawaska, New Brunswick
- Ste-Anne-de-Restigouche (also called Ste-Anne-des-Micmacs), Restigouche, Quebec
- Ste-Anne-des-Monts, Gaspé-Nord, Quebec
- Ste-Anne-de-la-Pointe-au-Père, Quebec
- Ste-Anne, Chicoutimi-Nord, Quebec
- Ste-Anne, Alma, Quebec
- Ste-Anne-de-la-Pocatière, La Pocatière, Quebec
- Chapel of Ste-Anne, Ilets Jérémie, Côte-Nord, Quebec
- Ste-Anne-de-Beaupré, Quebec
- Chapel of Ste-Anne, Ste. Marie de Beauce, Quebec
- Ste-Anne-d'Yamachiche, Quebec
- Ste-Anne-de-la-Rochelle, Shefford, Quebec
- Ste-Anne-de-Sabrevois, Iberville, Quebec
- Ste-Anne-de-Varennes, Quebec
- Ste-Anne-de-Roquemaure, Abitibi, Quebec
- St. Ann Shrine, Cormac, Ontario
- Ste-Anne-de-Hallébourg, Hearst, Ontario
- Ste-Anne-des-Chênes, Ste. Anne, Manitoba
- Lac Ste-Anne, Alberta

Bibliography

General

Aradi, Zsolt. *Shrines to Our Lady Around the World.* New York: Farrar, Straus and Young, 1954.

Boglioni, Pierre. "Pèlerinages et religion populaire au Moyen Age," 66-75, *Wallfahrt Kennt keine Grengen.* Munich: Schnell and Steiner, 1984.

Chelini, Jean, and Branthomme, Henry. *Les chemins de Dieu: Histoire des pèlerinages chrétiens des origines à nos jours.* Paris: Hachette, 1982.

Engelmann, Henri. *Le bâton du pèlerin.* Paris: Éditions S.O.S., 1982.

Hall, D. J. *English Mediaeval Pilgrimage.* London: Routledge and Kegan Paul, 1966.

Kendall, Alan. *Medieval Pilgrims.* New York: Putnam, 1970.

Labande, E. R. "Pilgrimages: Medieval and Modern," *New Catholic Encyclopedia*, New York: McGraw-Hill, 1967.

Laurentin, René. *Les routes de Dieu aux sources de la religion populaire: Pèlerinages, sanctuaires, apparitions.* Paris: Éditions O.E.I.L., 1983.

Littledale, R. F. "Pilgrimage," *Encyclopaedia Britannica*, Chicago: Werner, 1894.

Madden, Daniel M. *A Religious Guide to Europe.* New York: Collier, 1975.

McCarthy, M. C. "Pilgrimages: Early Christian," *New Catholic Encyclopedia*, New York: McGraw-Hill, 1967.

Nolan, Mary Lee, and Nolan, Sydney. *Christian Pilgrimage in Modern Western Europe.* Chapel Hill, NC: University of North Carolina Press, 1989.

Oursel, Raymond. *Pèlerins du Moyen Âge: Les hommes, les chemins, les sanctuaires.* Paris: Fayard, 1978.

Polan, S. M. "Pilgrimages in the Bible," *New Catholic Encyclopedia*, New York: McGraw-Hill, 1967.

Rowling, Marjorie. *Everyday Life of Medieval Travellers.* New York: Dorset Press, 1989.

"Les Sanctuaires Mariaux," 695-735, *Almanach populaire catholique,* 1988.

Santarelli, U. "Pilgrimages, Roman," *New Catholic Encyclopedia,* New York: McGraw-Hill, 1967.

Sigal, Pierre-André. *Les marcheurs de Dieu: Pèlerinages et pèlerins au Moyen Âge.* Paris: Armand Colin, 1974.

Stokstad, Marilyn. *Santiago de Compostela in the Age of the Great Pilgrimages.* Norman, OK: University of Oklahoma Press, 1978.

Sumption, Jonathan. *Pilgrimage: An Image of Mediaeval Religion.* London: Faber and Faber, 1975.

Turner, Victor, and Turner, Edith. *Image and Pilgrimage in Christian Culture: Anthropological Perspectives.* New York: Columbia University Press, 1978.

Wall, James Charles. *Pilgrimage.* London: Talbot, 1926.

Canada

Baran, Anna Maria. *Ukrainian Catholic Churches of Saskatchewan,* trans. by Christine Pastershank. Saskatoon: Modern Press, 1977.

Boglioni, Pierre, and Lacroix, Benoît. *Les pèlerinages au Québec.* Québec: Presses de l'Université Laval, 1981.

L'église de Montréal: Aperçus d'hier et d'aujourd'hui. 1836–1986. Montréal: Fides, 1986.

"Églises et sanctuaires," 331-386, *Almanach populaire catholique,* 1983.

Le grand héritage: L'église catholique et la société du Québec. Québec: Musée du Québec, 1984.

Laperrière, Guy. "Pèlerinages et pèlerins au Québec: Trois siècles d'histoire," 459-472, *Wallfahrt Kennt keine Grenzen.* Munich: Schnell and Steiner, 1984.

Leier, Heather, and Lozinsky, Joseph. *Mary as Mother: The Pilgrimage Shrines to the Blessed Virgin Mary in Saskatchewan, a Pictorial and Historical Approach.* Muenster, SK: St. Peter's Press, 1987.

Noppen, Luc. *Les églises du Québec: 1600–1850.* Québec: Éditeur officiel du Québec / Fides, 1977.

Pèlerinages canadiens: Monographies des principaux lieux de pèlerinage au Canada. Montréal: Imprimerie du Messager, 1928.

Pomedli, Michael, and Halmo, Joan. *Mary and God's People: Pilgrims on the Prairies.* Muenster, SK: St. Peter's Press, 1983.

Porter, John R., and Désy, Léopold. *Calvaires et croix de chemins du Québec.* Montréal: Hurtubise, 1973.

Porter, John R., and Trudel, Jean. *The Calvary at Oka.* Ottawa: National Gallery of Canada, 1974.

Robillard, Denise. *Églises et sanctuaires du Québec.* Québec: Tourisme Québec, 1984.

Sullivan, Kay. *The Catholic Tourist Guide.* New York: Meredith Press, 1967.

Thornton, Francis Beauchesne. *Catholic Shrines in the United States and Canada.* New York: Wilfred Funk, 1954.

Tremblay, Émilien. *The Epic of St. Ann in Western Canada.* Muenster, SK: The Prairie Messenger, 1971.

Varennes, Fernand de. *Lieux et monuments historiques de l'Acadie.* Moncton: Éditions d'Acadie, 1987.

Glossary

baldachino: A canopy projecting or suspended over an altar.

caryatid: A female figure used as a pillar to support an entablature.

entablature: The part of an order above the column, including *archtrave, frieze and cornice.*

ex-voto: Gift that was placed in the shrine as a witness to the favour received; for example, a crutch or brace or a home-made painting of a miraculous event.

mons gaudii: The hill of rejoicing from which the pilgrim first caught sight of the shrine.

reredos: An ornamental screen covering the wall at the back of the altar.

retable: Shelf or frame enclosing decorated panels above the back of the altar.

Scala Sancta: A series of steps that pilgrims ascend on their knees while saying special prayers.

scrip: The pilgrim's satchel or wallet.

triptych: Picture or carving on three panels, with side panels able to fold over the centre panel.

tympanum: The vertical triangular space forming the centre of a pediment, often carved.

Index